Welcome to the Sick Mind of a
SANE PERSON

Deconstructing Racism and White Supremacy

TERRY LEE WATSON

iUniverse books may be ordered through booksellers or by contacting:

iUniverse
1663 Liberty Drive
Bloomington, IN 47403
www.iuniverse.com
844-349-9409

Because of the dynamic nature of the Internet, any web addresses or links contained in this book may have changed since publication and may no longer be valid. The views expressed in this work are solely those of the author and do not necessarily reflect the views of the publisher, and the publisher hereby disclaims any responsibility for them.

Any people depicted in stock imagery provided by Getty Images are models, and such images are being used for illustrative purposes only.
Certain stock imagery © Getty Images.

ISBN: 978-1-6632-3021-8 (sc)
ISBN: 978-1-6632-3020-1 (e)

Library of Congress Control Number: 2022904309

Print information available on the last page.

iUniverse rev. date: 03/11/2022

"A sick mind made well is a stronger mind!"

Introduction

I once believed that America was a nation founded on the concepts of inalienable rights, truths, and liberties. Based on the evidence presented to me, I can see that these are merely nugatory proclamations. I allowed myself to believe in these concepts because they preserved the wellness of my mind. With my conceptual mind, I must acknowledge a bitter truth. As a black man in America, I must lie to myself constantly to keep my mind sane.

For whom are these liberties meant? Who can partake in the declaration of life, liberty, and the pursuit of happiness? A sane mind wonders.

I anticipate that some readers will push back on my interpretation of this robust bond. I prepare for those who move to heighten the concept of the word *pursuit* implying that this bond is not guaranteed, that these promises of rights are for only the pursuers. So please allow my sane mind to respond; this bond is neither inalienable nor a right.

That leads me to right now. Welcome to the sick mind of a sane person. I am the author and the moderator of this mind and the conductor of these excursions. This journey through this mind will reflect what I've seen and most important what I hope to see. I am aware that racism is not exclusive to black and brown bodies, but it is my black body in which my experiences lie; my black thoughts and consciousness are from where I speak.

Do not be surprised if you begin to realize that maybe it's not only my mind that has become sick. After all, I am not naive enough to believe that questioning racism and white supremacy are exclusive to my mind only. I am just the one to express it through the lens of sanity and sickness.

And with that said, enjoy this expedition.

Making of the Mind—The Race Edition

I write poems and critical thoughts during moments when I am not well. But believe me, I am well enough to describe, analyze, and process what is in front of me.

I realize that I was born sane. As a sane person, I have decided to record my reactions to and reflections on white supremacy as I've experienced it. When a black body honestly analyzes a black mind and realizes that a racially sedated consciousness is a part of his or her sanity, this mind can and more likely will become sick. Now that I know this, I can confirm that it is not an error when I write and what I write.

These experiences come in chaotic stories and occasional anecdotes followed by my disorderly yet manageable, compiled thoughts. Outbursts if you will. But I prefer it that way, and therefore, I record them as such. I label these outbursts as moments to remind myself that just as any sickness does, these too shall pass. Allowing these moments to pass without learning from them can result in cynical repetition. So with these moments, I am compelled to reflect on these experiences and hopefully make plans for a better future if not for myself, then for the next generation.

On to my first of many questions. What makes the mind sick? And more specifically, what role does white supremacy play in this sickness? Reacting to the chaos caused by white supremacy, and especially when the chaos is yours, can lead to a sick mind. Even though it can also expose the ailments of the mind, captioning these outbursts and acting as the conductor and passenger of such a mind allow for amazing reflections.

With the primary goal of deconstructing racism and white supremacy, I enable these reflections to present a portal to a greater understanding that will allow a pathway to sanity because I let it. I do this willingly, but it is exceedingly painful. To unshackle the mind is to bear free thought; it is to allow your God-given consciousness to break away from any inferiority complex and allow its strong sense of self-erudition. For example, let's take a look at the second question that led me to write. As a black man, how do I contribute to the sustainability of white supremacy? To my brothers, have you ever thought about that? Well, I have as you will see in my outbursts to follow.

It is not possible for a sane mind not to get sick once in a while due to the chaos that surrounds it and the new experiences that tend to remake it (only if we let it of course). I hope you have a few ways of getting your sane mind well, but if not, I hope my chaotic stories, occasional anecdotes, and compiled thoughts may offer a perspective that leads to your own remedy.

I write within my honest being. I live with the philosophy that there is no truth and that the most potent perception of reality remains untold. I chose to speak on the concept of racism first because my honest being compelled me to do so. Its cancer is lethal to our society, and if we were ever in need of a cure, it is now. In diagnosing my sick mind, I had to unshackle the greatness of white supremacy. This unshackling continues to be my most significant challenge as of yet.

With that, let us begin.

CHAPTER 1
THE WALK

TERRY LEE WATSON

A walk, as dreadful as the walk on Commerce Street.
I reckon my heart, but I felt no beat.
Water ashore this unprosperous feat,
I reckon my lungs, but I can't breathe.

Oh what land is this, eyes my brother to the north.
Oh what a sight this is propelled by an evil oar.
Thoroughly scorched, and spirit so weary,
A baby lost, mother's eye so teary.
Lord, strength doesn't know a will like this.
I take from this walk, this dreadful walk on Commerce Street.

What good do you take from the rights of my body?
What mends do you make from the past till now?
What good is a conscious that proclaims it is woke,
When it is capitalized ideologies leaves, you morally broke.

Oh, a walk, as dreadful as the walk on Commerce Street.

Crawling, Walking, and Running from Racism SR (Self-Reflection)

For decades, racial hate has been analyzed and theorized. Authors, social scientists, and theologians have kept a critical eye on the evolution and the sustainability of racism, a type of hate that is perplexing. Some see racism as the subset of white supremacy, some see racism as negative actions some do to others based on the pigment of their skin, and some don't see racism at all.

I had the opportunity to speak not only to those who see themselves as antiracist but also those who see themselves as reformed white supremacists. What stood out to me in my communication with them is not just their passion for eradicating the hate of racism but their methods of doing that. This I will discuss later; for now, I want to dive into one of my many thoughts about racism and hopefully address an important question: How do we recognize and move to end racism?

My first moment begins here!

I started to think about all the clichés that include the word *walk* and how it lends itself to the conversation about racism and the deconstruction of white supremacy.

First thought: You must crawl before you walk. A very common phrase. It is appropriate to begin this chapter (or this moment as I like to call it) titled "The Walk." It wasn't long ago that I took a walk down Commerce Street in Montgomery, Alabama. I visited this site for its historical excursion into the slave narrative.

Someone asked me a long time ago why I chose to talk about and ponder slavery, lynchings, Jim Crow, and other painful moments in black America's history. This I will disclose in the last chapter, but it should be known right now that I see my reflection on these moments as signs of strength and perseverance.

To understand this outburst and its reflections, I will recount my conversation with one of my white friends about this trip to Alabama and my intentions to visit some of the landmarks that hold America accountable for its treacherous history. My friend responded, "That seems like a lot of painful things to visit at once."

At that moment, I found that in white America, my sense of the walk, the steps necessary to deal with racism in our society, may be missing. What's more alarming is that I believe the same is valid with black America too. When it comes to taking the steps needed to face racism, eradicate this evil, and put to rest this construct that separates us, our sense and our willingness remain indivisible.

So regarding the phrase "You must crawl before you walk," when it comes to the painful walk of America's history, I realize that some people are not ready to walk and that most are not prepared or unwilling to crawl.

Second Thought: Reflection of the Crawl

What constitutes crawling? I analyze the crawl into four main points. First, you must invoke curiosity. Without curiosity, you will not have a need to crawl let alone walk. I focus on development because that is what I've studied. I think of my kid's journey as they began to crawl. Usually, kids are crawling to someone or something. My kids were no exception. They would crawl back and forth to my wife and me. Their curiosity was enough to will them from point A to point B. Whenever I talk about the epitome of hate, you will hear me say, "I'm intrigued" or "I'm curious why." I've chosen these words carefully because I understand this notion of curiosity and its role in exploration. Even in writing these reflections, I do so due to my curiosity about racial hatred. Why does someone choose to hate when there is so much opportunity for love?

The second thing that constitutes crawling is the willingness to set out and learn. Be careful, though. Do not set out to relearn or reinforce what you have come to understand. This is more important in Western civilization and especially in America. The history books, the depictions, and the personae are told by those who instilled racial hatred or did not see worthiness in us, and by us, I mean black bodies. These authors did not see black America as part of its pennant.

I had one of my first arguments in school with my history teacher. As a preadolescent, I refused to call George Washington the father of our country after I learned he had owned slaves, and as James Baldwin would say, "based on the evidence presented to me," I was not included in the notion of *our*. My African American blood could not allow me to call him the father of what I held dear and sacred—my country and my black body. I say this because it is essential to learn from those who loved us, from those who saw us as part of the *our*.

Third, be open to learning. Through the process of learning, you will come across the process of unlearning. This is inevitable but necessary. This you will find challenging and often painful. I know that from experience. However, you must be willing to unlearn as much as you are willing to learn.

We go through life defining our knowledge based on what we've learned. Imagine if we defined our knowledge based on what we've unlearned. As you will see in my stories, epilogue, and poems, this book is a collection of my unlearning material.

The fourth and final piece to the crawl is identifying your core. Identify your base because once you go through the walk, you may find it necessary to adopt or change your core. This can make a mind sick. Take time and identify your core. What do you believe is right? When you identify your core, you will have to decide on what you see as evidence of truth. You will have to conclude that you are the only one who can control this perception.

Going back to the analogy of the crawling baby, this fourth step is the difference between children discovering they have limbs to move versus finding out that they can control their limbs to make them move. After a while, muscle memory and visual coordination take over, and they become unaware of the control they have.

Identifying your core is just taking your mind to a spot not much visited. That place does not question only what you believe but also why you believe it and if it is acceptable to change.

Third Thought: Reflection of the Walk

Now that I have analyzed the crawl, what constitutes the walk? From time to time, I compare this process to the humanization process. Once you have decided to crawl, your vision should lead to walking. So just like the crawl, I analyzed the walk.

I recognized three things as the walk. First, you must go through with it and learn. This is the same as taking your first step. Curiosity has gotten you this far; now, decide to move on and learn. Just remember to pay attention to those you choose to learn from.

The next two steps are important as they begin to get at the core of a crucial step in tearing down the walls of white supremacy. Recently, I held a virtual forum on the topic of law enforcement addressing generational trauma in the black community. The panel comprised three black law enforcement professionals who were leaders of black law enforcement organizations. A question came from one participant about truth and reconciliation and the possibility of using that to address generational trauma. Quickly, each panelist echoed the same point: "I've been telling my truth my whole life and others before me. What has America done with that information?" Our participant even answered that question, "Nothing." I tell this story because it demonstrates the importance of the next two steps.

Reflection is the second thing important in taking the walk. Every time I find it necessary to unlearn something and replace it, I challenge myself by asking my reflection questions. Now that I have made these painful steps, what does it mean, and why is it important? Then I ask, What does it mean to me? Where has growth occurred? What did I learn?

How did I learn it? What am I going to do with this information? I find this step grows in importance as time goes on.

In the situation I mention above, what reflections has America made on the truth that my ancestors and forefathers gave this country? You will find in my many moments how the reflection of narratives by folks such as Frederick Douglass, Martin Luther King Jr., Malcom X, and many others seems to minimally exist in America's consciousness and heart; therefore, I am led to believe that America has yet to reflect.

Third and last, be willing to reidentify your core. I think this is something that doesn't happen as much as it needs to in America, and I might even be so brave as to state that it doesn't happen at all. I always say in my speeches and writing that we must humanize each other. But one detail that is important to understand in the humanization process is that in America, our history, our consciousness was not meant to humanize all. This is how on July 4, 1776, men could gather to sign a document that opens with "We hold these truths to be self-evident, that all men are created equal, that they are endowed by their Creator with certain unalienable Rights, that among these are Life, Liberty and the pursuit of Happiness" while still sustaining the evil institution of slavery.

With reidentifying your core, you will first have to understand that it may be tainted. Unless you unlearn what has been taught you, you will just find yourself seeking ways to reinforce and sustain the ideology of white supremacy. This most likely will lead to a sick mind, so make sure on your journey that you have ways to stay well and allow yourself to reflect, change, and check in with your core occasionally. Remember to ask the same questions you did before and see if your answers have changed. See if you believe the same thing or feel the same way. This is how we begin the humanization process.

Fourth Thought: Don't Talk the Talk if You Can't Walk the Walk

This is something I relay to anyone reading these reflections and then consciously deciding to begin this humanization process. No matter your identity, your voice is powerful. Use it, but be aware of the message you spread. Not everyone can walk the walk. Your message may be tainted and might spread the theology of white supremacy consciously or unconsciously. I have seen this. People I consider good natured in their unwillingness to unlearn wind up spreading their narratives and ideals, which in turn strengthens the institutions that oppress so many. I say this because I've done this, but I vow not to do so again.

I've spent a lot of time listening to people as you will see throughout my recaptured moments, and have seen this repeated time and again. The reason I appreciate people's narratives is that I like to see just how far they have walked if at all but most important, how much I can help them discover how much walking there is to do. I think it is important to let people talk as it may contribute not only to the development of their journey but to our own as well.

Fifth Thought: Walk It Off

This saying is typically associated with pain. I remember my coach years ago asking me, "Son, can you walk it off?" usually meaning, "Can you still play?" This is a great way to lead into checking in with yourself. Sometimes, you can walk it off, but sometimes, you are hurt or even injured and may need to sit a game out. That is okay. Whenever I choose to walk it off, I recognize two things. One, this game is significant to me and I do not want to be sidelined, and two, I can still go on. This is how I feel when I am talking about racism in some regard. Sometimes, I can go on knowing this game is too important to sit out, but nevertheless, I take time to realize that I still can go on. This is essential.

Sixth and Final Thought: Run, but Know When to Stop

If ever allowed my eyes to close, what thoughts will be allowed to run.
If ever allowed to rest at will, no, not until my last breath is done.

You will come across one of my poems titled "I Can't Afford to Be Tired." I read this poem at a Juneteenth event in 2021, the same year it became a federal holiday. What is monumental to me is not a president signing a paper making it law; it is the story of Opal Lee at age ninety-four seeing this come to pass.

When she was eighty-nine, Lee wanted to see Juneteenth become a federal holiday, so she marched and petitioned Congress to pass legislation making it a federal holiday. Make no mistake; she ran. But as inspiring as this story is, I am reminded that 1865 is a long way from 2021.

This leads me to my fine point. We find ourselves running. Thoughts and minds are running. Legs and motors are running. Tears and blood are running. All to achieve a world that some think already exists. Trying to leave behind a world better than we found it. With all that running, when can we stop? Most of us honestly don't know.

So to recap, you must crawl before you walk. In America, some people are not ready to walk, and most are not prepared to crawl.

Analyzing the Crawl

- Invoke curiosity.
- Have a willingness to set out and learn.
- Be willing to learn and unlearn.
- Identify and analyze your core.

Analyzing the Walk

- Go through with it and learn.
- Reflect on it.
- Reidentify and reanalyze your core.

Don't Talk the Talk if You Can't Walk the Walk

- Your voice is powerful, so use it, but be aware of the message you spread.
- It is important to let people talk as it may contribute not only to the development of their journey but also to yours.

Walk It Off

- Sometimes, you can walk it off, but sometimes, you are hurt or even injured and may need to sit a game out.

Now Run, but Know When to Stop

- With all that running, when can we stop? Most of us honestly don't know.

A Child's Play

During the eighties in a housing project, he was running to his door, a six-year-old black boy living in Queens, NY. Excited, he was running off the elevator toward the reinforced steel door marked 5D and banged on the door as loud as he could. (Some would call this the Po Po knock also known as the police knock.)

Bang! Bang! Bang!

How fitting it was that this pumped-up six-year-old was still excited from the NYPD's visit to his school that day. His mother came to the door and as always, asked, "Who is it?" while peeping through the peephole, but she could not see her child. Attempting to imitate a deep voice, the boy hollered, "*Police!*" Then there was silence.

Racism. A socially constructed means to divide power and instill fear.

The day the police officers came to this public school in Far Rockaway, this young boy was genuinely excited. "To protect and to serve"; that was how the sticker badges they handed out read. He wore that sticker all the way home admiring the shiny grey and blue NYPD logo on it. The paper hat constructed at the craft table fitted just right, so he wore that home too.

As he rode the bus home that afternoon, he came up with a plan that was sure to make his mother smile. At least he thought so. He would announce himself as a police officer when he arrived home. With his shield and paper hat, he was sure to pass as a miniature officer of the law and put a grin on his mother's face. He was six. What did he know about fear? It would not be long before his eyes would be pried open, but that day was a beginning moment of defining his core. His invoked curiosity allowed him to crawl.

Blink

The boy remembers those years all too well. He treasures them more than most would because they kept him relevant. God once put a precious gift in his heart, a gift of sanity, so remembering those moments was somewhat symbolic.

Let's start with the word *privileged*. Privilege as a concept was never explained to this young boy. After all, everything was a privilege. "You ate?" Privilege. "You slept under a roof?" Privilege. "You woke up today?" Praise God. Privilege! You get the idea. It's not until you lose a privilege or two that you start to realize what privileges truly are. That is what is so unique about race. This privilege cannot be gained or lost and is nontransferable therefore never allowing a shared perspective to take place. For example, the rich can lose their money and thus some privilege, but with race, a white person would never lose that privilege nor would a person of color gain that external privilege. It becomes crucial in my struggle to take the privilege I don't have, turn it into beacons of strength, and use the force to face the world.

For example, in the adult world, I find myself blessed. I get to travel and speak on topics near and dear to me. And occasionally, I will acknowledge the place and the space and the history in which I dwell. I may be presenting at an institution that I know was built on the genocide of its native people and constructed with the free labor of the Africans. In other words, my people. From this, I gain strength. Our society and institutions were never meant to include me, but here I am. Here I stand. No matter what oppression has been thrown at us, at me, I get to represent us. Most people will not get this, but I applaud those who do.

Blink

Fear is taught. My moments of sanity have made that concept very clear. A baby crawls to the edge of the bed without the fear of falling off. It approaches a hot stove without the fear of being burned. Parent teach their children to fear certain things to keep them safe. "No! Hot!" parents tell their children, who retrain their truth to accept this new fear.

Fear is taught to us for two primary reasons. First, it acts as our first safety mechanism as I explained above, and two, it helps us differentiate between comfort and anguish. We will move toward pleasure as we move toward safety, and we tend to run away from danger just as we do from pain. The division between fearful and fearless is decided on the direction you choose to move. Fear is an inevitable building block to feeling safe and comfortable. But what price are we willing to pay for safety? And for whom is comfort sustained?

Blink

Atrocities. I love that word. Not its meaning but in the spirit of describing what I have seen or come to understand. It is always good to express yourself and having the vocabulary to do so makes a narrative worth the telling.

The last time I was robbed at knifepoint, I laughed at my so-called robber. He must have thought I had cracked, and I might have. Thinking back, I should have responded differently considering the danger I was in, but that day, I just laughed. This begs the question, What can preteens have witnessed to make them so oblivious to such danger? My sane years. What bizarre times.

Eyes Shut Tight

TERRY LEE WATSON

Crack Bottles

On my block where this boy was raised,
He was amused by the crack bottles.
As a kid, he didn't know his ways.
But the days were spent collecting crack bottles.

Oh how the colors excited him,
Roy G. Biv, the collection so magnificent
In the rain, they would float. In the snow, they would soak … right in.

The properties of these capsule-size bottles were not a subject in school.
So as he experimented as a child, don't you subject him to a fool.
These were his crack bottles.

Seventy-one fifteen, there were plenty. The boy stored the bottles in a bag.
Reagan gave him cheese … and these crack bottles …
It was his hobby, each and every day, he would collect one and look at …
His crack bottles.

All around for him to see, no colors were too hard to find.
He once showed his mother his prize. She gasped and whipped his black
    behind.
And fear, genuine fear that he only saw once more spread across her face.
She stood directly over him, and then she began to pace.

"Boy," she said. "Do you know what the cops would do
If they found your crack bottles?
Do you know what they would say
If they found your crack bottles?"
As a child, he was not prepared for this adult world, nor did he fear.

"I would tell them, I did not steal them. These bottles are mine." I swear.

This was his collection.

No need to worry, no need for confession.

These are his crack bottles.

Where Does Empathy Go?

Filled with empathy, oh so young.
Filled with forgiveness, a new chapter's beginnings.
Now a moment of attempting to crawl …

A heavyset black boy leaves his home, and the lock clicks behind him as he walks down the hall toward the staircase. He is hungry, yet hunger has never stopped him before. The hallways are cold. Yet he is fearless of the elements that surround him and is ready to take on this new adventure that awaits him. During this journey, no one stops him to say, "Hi," "Hello," or "How are you?" As he descends five flights of stairs, no one pays attention to him, but he prefers it that way. If he were to engage in such a state, who knows what he would do? What he would say?

He waits behind the glass pane for the cheese-colored bus to take him to school. This visible glass does nothing to keep the cold out; it keeps the feeling of insecurity in. That day, the bus doesn't stop. It does not see the boy behind the glass. Is he invisible? Either way, the bus does not wait. Just like his sanity, it has left.

The boy thinks, *I cannot go back upstairs because only trouble will await me there.* He has decided. Without a jacket, a hat, bare soles, and gloves soaked through, he begins to take a short journey on foot to hop the A train. The boy wonders, *Why couldn't I be attending the school down the block?*

Twenty minutes or so later, he arrives at the last stop. Time to take the rest of this journey on foot. He knows this journey, this route, this routine. Another half-hour passes, and no one says "Hi," "Hello," or "How are you?" At last, he arrives late. All this for a day of a third-grade education.

Blink

I wonder how such a childhood impacts the social construct of race and the institution of racism it sustains. How does a person's experience influence his or her ability to show empathy? As an adult, I often think back to my childhood, a time when I still believed that we were all equal (or at least treated that way), that we were all included under the doctrine of "We the people."

My first untruth is formed in the concept of empathy or lack thereof. I was told that we were children of God and made in his likeness. I was told we were brothers and sisters in Christ. So with this, wouldn't it be easy to empathize? Wouldn't it be easy to ask, "How are you?"?

Blink

Back to that boy, that day ...

The boy remembers the multiple trips to school via the A train. His thoughts run on his rides to school: *Why did the bus refuse to stop on my street? I lived here my whole life. Why did no one talk to me? Then again, would I talk back?* It must be strange to see a young boy outside in winter without a jacket. Why did no one say anything? With age, does empathy begin to diminish? Did they empathize, or was this considered normal in his 'hood for people who looked like him?

Go ahead and argue with this child's construct of reality or perception. A sane mind would. A rational mind should.

He arrives late and walks through the doors of his public school recognized only by its number. The honor of a name was not meant for this school. He is unsure who first saw him, but he will never forget the first person who asks, "How are you?" that day. As he proceeds to the main office of this school, he keeps his head down wanting to avoid any lecture on why he is late or why he looks the way he does. *I don't want your pity*, the boy thinks. *Just give me my pass and let me go.*

He quietly opens the door, gives the late pass to his teacher, and takes his seat just in time for the bell to ring and for Mr. G to announce it's time for the gym. Mr. G! He likes Mr. G. He is a white Jewish teacher with a very thick mustache. Mr. G was the first teacher to tell this boy that he was too bright. That this boy did not belong in his special education class. His class was for those who struggled with academics. To Mr. G, the boy's academic abilities were advanced. His inability to make it to school on time and pay attention were the boy's downfall. That and the fact that this curious boy in all his unusual quirks could never get that social norm thing down.

Blink

In the mind of Mr. C, not Mr. G.

Today, I got up as normal and did my pre-workout routine. It was a cold one. It took me a while to find my scarf, but when I did, I grabbed it along with my water bottle and jolted out the door. I keep myself fit, and with my low-cut Kid-N-Play flat top, I know I still got it. But I am just a gym teacher, an elementary school gym teacher at that.

The school I work at has primarily black and brown children, so I guess it's good for them to see a black teacher once in a while. It is incredible what I can do for a child's self-esteem. Take today, for instance. I feel like I'm going to remember this day for a long time.

I leave the faculty office reserved for gym teachers and position myself to greet the kids as they run in from their multiple classes packed with energy and waiting on me to give them instructions for the day. I always have them line up on the tape, which I have stuck straight down in the middle of my gym. They know the routine, and they shuffle over and sit on the line. And as always, I walk down the line smiling at them all as they shout, "Good morning, Mr. C!" I respond, "Good morning to you too."

At the end of this line on this particular day, I see a boy. I don't remember his name, but I remember what he had on or failed to have on. Unlike the other kids, he is not sitting shoulder to shoulder. He is at least six feet away from anyone else. He refuses to look at me, but my gaze makes him aware that I'm looking at him because he starts to shake. And when I get close enough to him, he starts crying.

"Hey, what's the matter? What's wrong?" I ask.

As if this is the first time someone asks this question or shows empathy, he lifts his head and begins to cry louder. Now heads are turning, and the gym gets quiet. This causes him to put his head back down. This is not normal. I pull him out of the line, hold his hand, and ask him to walk with me to my office.

The boy's pants are very high, too high to cover his sockless ankles. His T-shirt is too big. Too big to stay on his shoulders. And his sneakers, not attached to the soles, allow his big toe to show on this frigid day. I escort him to my office. "How are you?"

Before the day is through, I stitch up his shoes to cover his big toe, a skill I learned from my father. A gym teacher who can repair shoes—a cliché, I know. I ask around to see if we can find him a coat. The boy tells me that he walked from the A-train to school in his current condition. We can't have that. We find a coat in the lost and found unclaimed for two years and give it to him. He doesn't say thank you, but he doesn't have to. How can I be the only adult to do something? Where has empathy gone?

Blink

The boy wonders, *Did Mr. C see himself in me today? Or maybe he takes time to look at each child every day?* Although the boy did not admit it then or since, he may have wanted empathy from the beginning. Even as a young child, he realizes it is simple to feel compassion for others. But the question still plays on his consciousness, *Where does empathy go?*

Blink

What role does empathy or the lack thereof play in sustaining racism? As I mentioned previously, curiosity and the openness to take the necessary steps to eradicate racism is key in deconstructing white supremacy. However, the inability to empathize will surely stop someone from invoking curiosity and will never allow for an openness to learn.

I speak about empathy a lot in my work. I understood early on that if you empathized with your neighbors, you would want to protect their homes because part of you would see their homes as part of yours. You would want to protect their well-being because you would see their well-being as part of your own.

Blink

Let might be the humane struggle, and watch my strength become overbearing.

Caring for a stranger as a brother is what I was told is God fearing.

But swearing, maybe one day, this empathy will be still, and its intentions are guileless and within goodwill.

Tell empathy to come, and to stay, and to be. Stable as the rock protruding from a dolor sea.

Find me empathetic because I know when it's lost. The sting from a child in bitter frost.

If I can find empathy, then to you, I say, "Take in." Say, "How are you?" to the human within.

Eyes Shut Tight

Wanted

I remember vividly the first time I was called a nigger as a child, as vividly as the last time I was called that despicable word three decades later. I remember each time this vile word was used to challenge my worth or that of those I loved. I title this part of my sane years as "Wanted."

I was told they did not want me here; my acceptance was not granted.
My mind's eye stayed watery, burry, and slanted; vision cut off from the
    promissory land.
I was told that my presence was scary. My entrance was not granted.
I can see from a distance, but never inside was I allowed. That was not for
    me as it was not for my ancestors.
Look around here. I find myself here but never wanted.

My curiosity has gotten me this far, but never has it allowed me to break
    the skin that is in. Always taunted.

My story is used until its value is diminished. My voice is misplaced and silenced here, where I am never wanted. I've walked until I was left to crawl constantly aware of the eggshells that surrounded me. Something had to crack—either me or a shell—but these eggshells are forever wanted.

From the crack, we blossom today surrounded by the weeds from a daunting path. Our voice will give meaning to our existence, power to ourselves, our people, and we will shout, "You are wanted here at last!"

Look around here. You may find yourself here and indeed needed. Your perseverance has gotten you this far. Just crawl a bit farther to break that skin that is in. Never defeated.

Your story is used. Take time to be replenished. Your voice is influential in the space in which you are needed. Once you've walked, never crawl again. Crush all eggshells that threaten your well-being. If you crack, let it be done to bear new fruit. New fruit is needed too.

We will feed a new generation from your new fruit and pave for them a new path that is less daunting. Their voice will give meaning to our existence, power themselves, their people, and this new generation will shout out, "I was always wanted here!"

Abroad

One of the most incredible experiences black men in America can have is visiting their homeland. Their motherland. Africa! Second to that is leaving the land they call home, America.

Recently, I traveled to the UK and spoke with a young woman who identified my American, New York accent and asked me, "How does it feel being black and living through the era of Trump? Are you scared?"

I paused for maybe a little too long, but I wanted to answer this question correctly. I wanted to relay my feelings about America as a whole, and I didn't want to give number 45 or any president credit for those feelings. As in my sane moments, I ponder a while before saying, "I feel the same as I do any other time in America. You see, for years, I've been telling people about the racism and bigotry that still exist even more so after electing a black president. If racism is as American as apple pie, 45 is just following the recipe."

After I left this conversation, I thought about it for a while. I knew this stranger was making small talk. My statement to her more than likely would be forgotten in fifteen minutes. But that is not why I said it. I wasn't trying to make an impact on her. I was reflecting for myself. No one can create something that's already there; people can either partake in it or do their part to destroy it.

One of the biggest misconceptions about racism is that racism is achieved by acting a certain way or doing something. However, it is just as achievable as failing to do something.

Humble Am I

Humble mind, find peace
Let my peace of mind be free
Mind my freedom cry

My moments of saneness come usually right before the moment I attempt to seek peace. However, before this moment of peaceful consciousness, I find myself in a state of mind that I am sure some can identify with. I title this haiku "Humble Am I" because I see humility as an inevitable state to maintain sanity as a black man. The famous poet Langston Hughes spoke of the humbleness of being black and conveniently connected the adjectives of docile, meek, and kind. This he said to America as a warning.

A wondering mind wonders …

What evil ideology makes a man's sanity entwined with his humbleness while living in a boisterous land that shouts freedom and bravery? If my home is loud, then should not my right to remain sane?

A wondering mind wonders …

If I can only be humble, what opportunities do I have to find worth within my boisterous home? What is the opposition to me being free and having this peace of mind?

A wondering mind wonders …

What do I owe a homeland that upholds bravery and freedom but humbles me to keep me submissive?

This is my freedom cry.

When I was a child, my grandmother told me, "Honey, never talk about yourself. Let others talk about what you do. Remain humble." However, one thing is missing from that piece of advice: telling your truth. I always saw humbleness as a good thing, and in some regards, I still do. But humbleness requires silence, and sometimes, silence is not an option for people who were made to be invisible. I began by saying my moments of saneness came right before I attempted to seek peace. Whenever I experience something traumatic either close or afar by distance or time, there is that moment when I grieve followed by undo sadness and anger, but after that, I start to look for answers. Why did this happen? How? What exactly happened? This is the moment I speak of. After I have processed such tragedy, I enter the realm of sanity to ask questions. To receive the answers to those questions, I must be humble. This is what I call a plan to heal.

Not long ago, I had an interaction with my son. As brilliant as my kids are, I need to instill things in them that I consider sacred. As their father, I know they will develop into their own persons. I want them to think freely and always possess curiosity, but I also want them to understand humbleness and its place. I am blessed to have a son on the autism spectrum, and frankly, being as brilliant as he is, humility does not come so easily to him nor does its understanding.

He recently said that he was frustrated because he felt others did not understand his point of view on a particular subject. He said, "Dad, I know this material. Why's everyone else taking so long to learn it?"

"Honey, be humble," I told him.

"Why?"

I just looked at him. I didn't have a legit answer for that.

I knew that not showing humbleness would lead to his not being liked or appreciated in this class, but I also knew that my son didn't care. I knew he cared about right and wrong, true and false, up and down. To him, being liked is not necessary (as he constantly reminds me). So I asked him, "What do you hope to achieve?"

"What do you mean?"

"Well, what is your purpose in this course? In life?"

"I don't know," he said.

I spoke about how education led to opportunity. I explained the same thing that had been demonstrated to me growing up. It's not just what you know but whom you know. It's not just what you do but your method of doing it.

He looked up at me and said something that led to this great reflection: "If I'm capable, why is it important that I be likable?"

We act or behave differently to be accepted even if that behavior diminishes our capabilities and chips away at the sanity we hold so dearly. Why? I recently posted on social media about my inability to code switch., to present an illusion of whiteness, intentionally or unintentionally creating a persona to hide my blackness. I may have tried to act differently to be accepted, but I've failed horribly. Therefore, I've abandoned this notion. I speak with friends and coworkers in the same way I speak at home. As I gain information, I may change my approach or what I say, but that change is developmental and available to everyone. I am not ignorant of the fact that abandoning this notion may lead to fewer opportunities, but in my son's words, "Why is that important?"

Why do I speak about humbleness in regard to racism? Modesty has its place in our society. However, I tend to question what impact humility has on sustaining the institutions of oppression for my people. You know, throughout this excursion through my mind (sick and well), my questions always remained inward. My questions are proposed with self-reflection. For example, *How do I …? How can I …?* and so on because I see my passion for the humanizing process as a legacy I can leave the next generation. And in the process of humanizing, as I mentioned earlier, we must be willing to crawl and walk by analyzing ourselves and by questioning the intentions of those who demand humility from us. If we are to pass on any legacy, it must be through this form, one constructed not through the lens of the consciousness that seeks to dehumanize us but through the lens that demands that our being is needed.

These intentions are to pass on a legacy representing our country's promise versus its behaviors and actions thus far. And yes, I see these two things as different. I observe a country that strives for freedom and liberation for all but instills and maintains institutions that hinder this goal in its ideals and practices. I've witnessed a divide that is noticeable and accepted by all. So if my mind and my actions just by their mere presence move this country toward its promissory decree, humbleness I fear may be out of my reach. Humbleness can extract from the progress of justice thus far and contribute to a sick mind as well.

So through my humbleness, mind my freedom cry.

TERRY LEE WATSON

Walking to Running: Entering the Mind of White Supremacy

It is time to walk, no run
Time to let your mind go free
Run to freedom land

Do not take any of these reflections as cynical ideology or an unpatriotic stance. Nothing is further from the truth. Instead, recognize them for what I say they are—my journey to learn and unlearn, reflect, and reidentify my core. My question: What does it take to explore a sane mind made sick?

The most extraordinary story of American patriotism is the story of the runaway slave. It is easy to proclaim and fight for a free country when the country's freedom stance has always included you. But to be a part of a free civilization in bondage and then to risk your life says more to the striving for freedom than any other American narrative. I believe this fortitude still exists among black Americans.

This is not a book about history, but historical significance is always worth exploring. The funny thing about historical exploration, however, is that it discloses what some overlook or tend to neglect. This notion of historical neglect intrigues me, and this is how I will begin this reflection. What we neglect to see as we run.

Not long ago, I came across the story of Archibald Dixon, a US senator from Kentucky who owned slaves. I understand he wasn't the only one. In fact, out of the first eighteen presidents, twelve were slave owners. I came across the book *History of Missouri Compromise and Slavery in American Politics* written by his wife. She painted a picture of the "happiest class of laboring people the world has ever known (p. 240)."[1] What really is astonishing to me is that she, entitled to her truth, presented evidence of how slaves were when they were "protected" by her husband, Archibald, versus when they were free. She explained that after Archibald died in 1876, freed slaves attended his funeral and paid their respect. They—the newly free Negroes once slaves—shed "tears of genuine grief."

As I thought of this, I remembered the narratives of slaves who had escaped their "protectors," who wouldn't understand why, like Dixon. After all, we dressed these slaves well, fed them well, and even allowed them to get paid well on some occasions. If this does not convince you of my good nature, ask my slaves, and they would offer words of respect and ensure that I, their master, is benevolent. This is one of the most incredible tricks of white supremacy that I will outline in the section titled "The Legacy and Legend That Is White Supremacy." But for now, I want to demonstrate what my version of reflection looks like.

Blink

As I explored the narratives of the runaway slave, I had to examine the records of the slaveholder. Crawl, walk, run.

I allowed myself to learn about the consciousness of slave owners through their self-proclaimed benevolent sense. Crawl, walk, run.

After all, this is how they saw themselves, and this is where I allowed my sane mind to visit. Crawl, walk, run.

---

[1] Dixon, Archibald, Mrs., 1829-1907. History of Missouri Compromise And Slavery In American Politics: a True History of the Missouri Compromise And Its Repeal, And of African Slavery As a Factor In American Politics. 2d ed. Cincinnati: R. Clarke Co., 1903.

The Vista of Mrs. Dixon

The viciousness that is said to have taken place in slavery is an outliner and unusual. Discipline was used only when necessary. No reasonable man would punish his slaves for no good reason. That is preposterous. But more so, it was for the benefit of those slaves who needed protection. I will not allow such consciousness to conclude that my husband, a representative of a union that proclaims equality, held from the Negro unalienable rights. All our slaves were grateful for what we provided them and how we treated them. We treated them like family. They were family. I don't have to make peace with myself. I treat my slave well sometimes putting my slave's well-being before my own as long as it doesn't significantly impact our superiority.

We allow ourselves to be their protectors and acknowledge that the slaves, as in need of protection (whispers to self) *even though we are in a position of power to dismantle the system in which security would be needed.* They are joyful, and we are so glad to be their protectors. That is all that matters.

Eyes Shut Tight

Ideology of the Invisible Man

What I see, what I see, no judgment, please
From what I see
If what I see is a struggle for power
Then what I see is inequality

Do see me, do see me, no judgment please
For what you see.
If the color of my skin is invisible to you,
Then what you see is really not me.

My struggle, so real
Your opinion, so not
Your history, I remembered
My history, I forgot

Seek, and you will find
Our future is far behind
My conscious is awoken and true
Destined to lie miles beyond you.

Invisible as I may be,
The world view is not complete without me
When my light ceases to be lit
These words you will know and never forget.

Why Does Racism Prevail? ASKing for a Friend

Why is it hard to stop racism? How does racism prevail? Ever thought about it? I mean, seriously thought about it?

Enter a room with a group of people with either a heterogeneous or homogeneous racial background and ask, "Are you a racist?" I have done this a couple of times. The majority if not all would be offended and proclaim that they were far from it. Those who answered yes would do so only because they thought it was a trick question and wanted to stand out as progressive, recognizing privilege. In this space of contradictory truths and untruths, you begin to hear all the ways of presenting the nonracist self. Some (thanks to the brilliant minds like Dr. Kendi and his book *How to be an Antiracist*) would start to demonstrate ways they practice being antiracist.

I did this before with a smaller heterogeneous racial group and still remember all the responses I received as if it were yesterday. The question I proposed was a simple question requiring a simple yes or no, no explanation needed. Nevertheless, the narratives presented themselves—a willingness to run away from the notion of racism always. Some are unable or unwilling to take the steps to understand the underpinning in which racism so comfortably resides. I will talk about how I deal with these narratives in the next moment titled "The Spectrum of Racism." But for now, the question remains, How does racism prevail if it is so disposed? The question I tend to ask along with "Are you a racist?" is "Does racism exist in your community?" I get mixed responses when I ask that, but the consensus is that racism still exists. So if no one is racist and everyone despises racism or at the very least speaks against it, how can racism prevail?

After reflecting on this, I have a theory. I call it the ASK theory of racism. I model this after the hiring practices known as KSA—knowledge, skills, and attitudes (or abilities). The funny thing about it is that without the KSAs at a job, you will be deemed incompetent. Some say that it was essential first to prove your knowledge and then your skills and have an attitude of competency. So let this reflect on what is necessary to eliminate racism.

If racism is a disease, America has used malpractice to treat it. The malpractice of the treatment of racism can easily be explained by looking at practices used by a doctor to treat sick people. Let's say you're sick, God forbid, and you go to the doctor. When you arrive at your doctor's office or call to make an appointment, what is the first thing you're asked? "What's wrong?" Your answer to that is crucial. It allows the doctor to define what is wrong, come up with an accurate prognosis and diagnosis, and provide the correct treatment. Well, with racism, that doesn't happen. If your doctor's office were to follow the procedure used to deal with racism, it would look like this.

You call your doctor's office and say, "I'm not feeling well."

Your doctor responds, "That doesn't mean you're sick. It can be anything. Are you sure you need a doctor?"

When dealing with racism and the historical trauma it has dealt, those who can participate in eliminating racism are not ready to engage. As I mentioned earlier, some are not prepared to walk, and some are not prepared to even crawl.

"I believe I may have the flu," you say.

"That can't be the case because we offer flu shots, and if you got one, you could not possibly have the flu."

When someone of color points out that the sickness of racism is present and impacts them, we are given narratives of the current conditions that in theory eliminate any thoughts that racism is prevalent or at a minimum not relevant to the sickness.

Now please do understand that for most people, this conversation will end. I mean, who would continue to have this conversation with no evidence of a solution in their sane minds? But this is a pivotal point to understand. In America, black people are expecting to continue this conversation, and whenever this conversation is not to continue because we do not see a cheerful ending to it, we are then being difficult or perpetuating the stereotype of the angry black man or woman.

However, let's say that you're willing to work through the sickness to come to healing; your response may be, "Doctor, I didn't get the flu shot for this or that reason." If your doctor were to continue this malpractice, his or her response would be, "That sounds like an excuse. You had the same opportunity to get the shot everybody else had."

Oppression is sustained when the oppressed are told how oppression should be viewed or dealt with. The malpractice I speak of is the malpractice that has been common knowledge and practice in our society so far.

How is this presented?

"What about black-on-black crime?"

"Why aren't you protesting that? Why are they rioting?"

"Why are they acting like thugs?"

And then the whole bootstrap analogy ...

The malpractice of racism is the key factor in its current existence. Because we cannot accurately treat racism like the disease it is, it prevails.

Now back to the KSAs of racism.

Let's say you're applying for a job as an electrical engineer. You would have to show that you possess the knowledge required to handle the job, that you understand the theories and know what's necessary for you to do the job.

Next, you would have to show that you possess the skills required. You would bring up your internships, previous employment, apprenticeships, and so on.

Once you've establish your skill set, you have to show you have the right attitude to do the job. Every day, will you come to work with the "I'm here to get the job done, and I'm going to do the best I can"? You may possess the knowledge and skills, but your competency will be negatively impacted if your attitude is in the wrong place.

However, the KSAs of racism are in reverse. So maybe more appropriately, they are the ASKs of racism. Racism prevails because of the lack of ASKing. So first, you need to have to right kind of attitude to deal with racism. I've covered that—the willingness to crawl, walk, and run to eliminate racism. Without the right attitude, you will never begin developing any skills or knowledge necessary to end racism. Without the proper perspective, you wouldn't see the journey as a necessity.

If you have the right attitude, you'll be able to engage. During the engagement, you can begin to develop the skills to deal with racism. Just as with any craft, practice is needed to reach perfection. I understand that not everyone is ready to engage especially if they do not have the right attitude. However, once you have engaged, you can develop knowledge of why racism prevails. Once you know that, you can begin to fight against systems in which racism so comfortably resides. The reason I mention the ASKs of racism is because it is a model for engaging. We have moved away from engagement (for some of the reasons I mention in the malpractice thus far) allowing racism to prevail.

So back to the questions, Why is it hard to stop racism? How does it prevail? Quite simply, it is hard because we make it, and it prevails because we willingly and otherwise allow it.

The Spectrum of Racism

Racism and racist! I've had a long time to think this over. No one really likes to be called a racist or to be accused of racism. These terms have become highly disregarded in our culture. There are different levels of racism. Maybe we have looked at the identity of racism inaccurately or at the very least incompletely.

The following theory proposed on racism should be seen as a spectrum, a level of mentality that impacts the functioning of our world. Like most spectrums, it can be represented by a bell curve. I believe I placed the five phases appropriately, but I cannot show statistical proof, so for now, a theory will have to do.

A: Consequential racist/racism: I place the consequential racist low on the bell curve. This is the racist most people think of. People or groups who believe that their race is superior to others and are willing to commit violent acts to sustain their ideology. Does a group or individual come to mind?

B: Noncommittal racist/racism: I place next on the bell curve the noncommittal racist. I will discuss this level as well as the others in greater depth, but for now, you should know that the noncommittal racist/racism would be people or groups that deny the existence or the impact of racism in society.

C: *De minimis* racist/racism: I place the de minimis racist on the middle level. This level of racism describes most civilizations at this time. I can see the argument for level D to be placed here, but I believe that the majority of our population would identify here.

This de minimis racist/racism would be people or groups who acknowledge that racism exists and has a negative impact on society but do not believe its impact is significant enough to require additional action or acknowledgment.

D: Despondent racist/racism: Past the de minimis level, we start to see a more conflicting outlook. The despondent racist/racism would be described as people or groups highly discouraged by racism in society. Despondent racists are possibly those who verbally stand against racism because it impacts their well-being.

E: Racist/racism combatant: I am very comfortable saying that a tiny population in any society would fit in this level. Racist/racism combatants are people or groups who would stand up against racism or a racist even if it meant putting their freedom, well-being, safety, or even lives in jeopardy.

Despondent racists may stand against racism, but racist combatants will always stand up against it because they identify racism as a root of the problem. Despondent racists would stand up against racism as long as it doesn't negatively impact them, while racist combatants would risk their lives to fight racism.

So why is it important to understand the different phases? The answer to that is a question: How can we begin to engage if we are not willing to provide a reasonable understanding? Remember back to the "Why does racism prevail?" question? I talked about the heterogeneous racial group in which I proposed the question, "Are you a racist?"

I'll put some context to this. The people who attend these presentations are aware of the topic, so the background is transparent. However, when I ask the question, I do so at the beginning of a presentation so the audience is unaware of where I am going with the question. I'll ask the question and then scan the room. Silence … I monitor the room until someone speaks up. Talk about awkward silence. Once someone does break the ice, it is usually met with a "No" or "No, I am not."

I respond with "*Hmmm*" or an "Okay" followed by more awkward silence. This is when the narratives come.

"I'm married to a _____"

"I've always admired Dr. King."

"I believe we all bleed the same color, red."

And my all-time favorite, "I was raised not to see color."

You get the point.

Let me take a step back. What most people tend to do here is try to convince a stranger, a black stranger at that, that they're not racist. Are you a racist? That's a closed question but with an open, self-reflective, dialogue possibility. When I allow silence to occur, I enable folks to self-determine why they are not racist.

Taking another step back, I also know (because I've asked) what is going through their minds when that question is asked. The characteristics of a racist must be clear before you can define yourself as a nonracist. And as I just mentioned, most people think of the consequential racist. They think, *If I don't fit that model, I'm not racist.*

Let me reanalyze a previous question through the spectrum of racism.

Why does racism prevail? Most people spend time and energy trying to prove they don't fit in the mode of the consequential racist. Once they have determined that, they allow the world to continue. Even if they recognize the harmful impact racism has, their consciousness will enable them to lose interest in change allowing curiosity and empathy to join their consciousness and losing the will to run, walk, or crawl.

How does racism prevail? It survives well in a climate filled with consequential, noncommittal, and de minimis people. In this world, it causes a despondent mind to pause and not act. Who is willing to be a combatant when their peace is ingrained in this environment? This is why I put the combatant low on the curve. There is no peace for a combatant when racism is around because racism is an evolutionary branch of injustice, and for my combatant people, there is no peace if there is no justice.

Finally, how does racism prevail? To put it plainly, we don't examine how comfortable we allow ourselves to become with racism. And we don't let ourselves look at how we have allowed ourselves to participate in that spectrum through that comfort. We are fixated on the action not to deter the importance, but we ignore our condolence of the systems that sustain consummated evils of racism.

The Journey Home Is Long

Opportunity bound,
this journey should not be long.
Its distance should not be great.
Opportunity found,
its founders should be strong.
Its strength should pull its weight.
This land of opportunity promises finders much
But its reality remains woefully out of touch.
My skin may not let me in
My brown may be turned down.
If I forever am persistent, a denier resistant
Then might this opportunity be mine as well
Let me take this journey and duly tell.

Opportunity bound,
This journey will be long
Its distance will be great
This foundation will not be strong
Taking this journey excepting its fate.
This land may not promise me much
I live in reality and remain indeed in touch
My skin will not break
My brown will always be around
I am the will of persistence, a genuine denier resistant
And if I find such opportunity, well,
I promise to keep its gates open and use my strength to pry its cell.
So soon, I may see you taking this journey's trail.
This journey is indeed long.

The White Ally

There is always so much to worry about, ponder, and explore. I sometimes feel that this is all I do and therefore never reach that moment of sanity I crave. Have I allowed my imagination and perseverance for hope to cloud my ability to be stable?

Spending time collecting narratives and my thoughts on them has been enlightening, time well spent indeed. Each record gives meaning and perspective to the questions I ask. I remember one conversation that got me thinking about race and racism in America. I have deep discussions about race, racism, and injustice in general with my friends. Some of these conversations are in line with how white people can address racism, and some are in line with how black people can deal with the trauma of racism. However, there is one piece of information I find myself repeatedly giving to white allies.

In a conversation with someone I consider a friend, I said, "White people need to become comfortable speaking to other white people about racism." My friend gave me a somewhat puzzled look, which prompted me to repeat the statement.

Often, I'm asked about allyship; what does allyship look like to me? What role does allyship play in the fight against racism? How can an ally intervene? These are the most common questions I get about allyship. I just covered the spectrum of racism and my theory on how racism prevails.

If you take nothing else from this walk, make sure you take away this. Your allyship should not be grounded in sustaining the trauma racism brings. As important as it is, your allyship should work to replace, not repeat, the trauma. Dealing with racism does not mean continuing the trauma that racism brings. Let's not contribute to the sick mind but contribute to its healing.

One way of doing this is to be mindful of when you show allyship.

TERRY LEE WATSON

Do not show allyship only in the presence of your black friend; also offer allyship when your black friends are not around. White allies, get comfortable talking to your white friends, family, church members, and coworkers about racism.

Why Can't I Feel?

If sorrow is all I have, then the world is grey

If song is sung in minor key only and no one to show the way

Why can't I feel?

Have my eyes seen too much? Has my heart been crippled with repetition
without crutch?

Why can't I feel?

Is the sun unable to cast light, although it shines?

A single prayer sent with vigor, to leave a dark shadow behind.

Why can't I feel?

Is it because of the fear? Knowing if I dare to feel, it could lead to greater
despair? Living constantly aware of all other possibilities.

The bad, the ugly, and the despicable. It's what I fear.

Why can't I feel?

Tell me its traumas are due, drama to the highest level, drag over time and
too easy to pursue.

Feeling is an entity made a privilege, and my privilege has been provoked.

Why can't I feel?

TERRY LEE WATSON

Black and Sick

To what do I owe a tired body and a sick mind?

The question I always asked. Is it worth my energy or my sanity?

To continue to crawl, walk, or run. To my tired body. When will it rest?

To my tired mind. Will there still be space to run?

Is being black and sick America's new addiction?

Like Tulsa, left to crumble and burn.

Or will America treat us like Tuskegee and hold onto the remedy and watch to see what a people will do?

Talk to me now. My mind is tired of waiting for an answer that is never to come. What do you get from this sick, America?

What new commerce have you thought of now? What is your message for me now? Are you here to convince me that my sick mind is an illusion? Is this your conclusion of what a sane black mind looks like?

I am searching and reaching for the tranquility of mind now. I am looking to get over it and not pass on this sickness. My sane mind tells me it is time to dislodge this onerous baton from this generational relay of tribulation. America, my black peacefulness can no longer depend on your goodwill.

America, my black consciousness can no longer depend on the inspection from your superiority complex.

I've crawled, walked, marched, and I continue to run. Fought, prayed, protected, and some. Now, it is time for my mind to be well. Not tomorrow, not later, but now.

Know this America, whatever you gained from my black sick mind, I'll be taking it back.

CHAPTER 2
THE AMERICAN CELEBRATION

Oh, come take part in this American celebration
Oh, say can you see the freedoms of this land
Come, take part in this American celebration
Celebrate this greatness hand in hand

Come smile, come laugh, embrace my joy
Come young man, old lady, girls, and boys
Detest and protest any inequities for the unknown
Even if these inequities are found to be homegrown

Come meet under the banner that is red, white, and blue
Its colors may be the same, and its design woven through
I relished in my blessings, and I accept what is to come
No matter who you are or where you come from

Oh, come take part in this American celebration
Celebrate this greatness with us, hand in hand

I learn lessons in life as we all should. When I was twelve, I was paid $20 for forty hours of work. Lesson learned—Never take on a job until you know how much you'll get paid.

However, some lessons learned are not as simple. I must warn you that the questioning of the mind truly begins now as do its lessons. I will tell you that from here on out, at this moment, titled "The American Celebration," you can begin to understand how a sane mine can become sick.

The picture you see here introducing this moment is famous. I use it in an activity called lynching or American celebration. What is fascinating about this particular picture is that people have a difficult time distinguishing between the two based on the facial expressions and the joy the photographs present. The question I asked myself in preparation of this activity was, What's the relevance of the destruction of black bodies and minds to the satisfaction and well-being of America?

A couple of years back, I attended a Fourth of July celebration with my wife and kids. I celebrate the independence of our country and the symbolization of freedom and liberty. During this celebration, I saw the same faces smiling, laughing, joking, eating, and celebrating. I had a flashback to the picture above. I then thought about the famous speech given by Frederick Douglass in 1852 titled "What to the slave is the fourth of July?" Since I became aware of this speech, the Fourth of July has become for me the saddest day of the year. It is an annual reminder of what America should be, could be, but refuses to be. But my mind does not stop there.

At the beginning of this book, I said there were two reasons I decided to write. One being to answer the question what makes the mind sick? But I also tend to answer the question as a black man, how do I contribute to the legacy of white supremacy? I took some time to think about that. And as I remember the independence of a country that does not see me worthy of independence, I wonder what other celebrations I partake in that contribute to this institution of white supremacy. Columbus Day? Christmas? Thanksgiving? New Year's? Even Martin Luther King Jr. Day?

That is information that could make the mind sick. If you grew up in an American school, you were taught of the greatness of Dr. Martin Luther King Jr. You learned about his philosophy, his famous "I have a dream" speech, and his perseverance when it came to upholding the ideology of nonviolence through one of the most violent times in our country. You learned about his sacrifice for the consciousness and soul of this country.

When I was a kid, just his name instilled pride in me. But through these many moments of reflections, I have come to wonder why we celebrate Martin Luther King Jr.'s Day so vividly but practice as a nation actions more congruent with the teachings of Malcolm X? Why isn't there a holiday memorializing the contributions to the honorable minister

Malcolm X? If we as Americans are to sing the words to the Toby Keith song "The Courtesy of the Red, White, and Blue," and I quote, "'Cause we'll put a boot in your ass, It's the American way," doesn't that more closely align with the teachings of Malcolm X than of Martin Luther King Jr.? To say "put a boot in your ass" the same as "by any means necessary"? If we as a country truly believed in the ideology to turn the other cheek or nonviolence, we wouldn't have fought so many wars or imprisoned so many people.

Please do not consider my statements as a call to be unpatriotic; in contrast, it is patriotism that I seek. Please do not make my remarks as a call to choose one ideology over another. My intent is not to influence your understanding of injustice and not to point out the hypocrisy but to show you what can lead to a sick mind when analyzing racism in America.

So back to the American celebration. At this time, I don't want to go into great detail, but I do intend to outline what it took for me to disengage from the perspective of such a mind. I take this action to make my mind and America well.

Forthcoming on the Fourth

1. December 16, 1773, Boston Tea Party
2. March 23, 1775, Patrick Henry, "Give me liberty or give me death."
3. June–July 1776, Declaration of Independence.

There was no party for us in 1773. No independence in '76, but today, we are fixed on celebrating this cause decoration.

America, what is your conviction to show us your independence today?

While your bombs burst in the air, my greats were given America's perilous terrorizing fear.

From the home of the brave, it should be noted

"No refuge could save the hireling and slave

From the terror of flight and the gloom of the grave."

How great a land is America to me? Great enough to dismantle my people's consciousness and dignity.

What is our freedom worth in the land of the free? Mind my cynical thoughts.

I asked this as I am forthcoming on the fourth.

What is your conviction to show your independence today?

Is it the,

Sweet tea sipping on strange-fruit Sundays,

Or the

Mountaintop speaking on mundane Mondays

Twisted is my mind, may this Tuesday bring.

A terrain so peaceful, just a Wednesday fling

I trust that Thursday last not long in my sick thoughts.

Allow my mind, its freedom, my wellness well fought.

49

Frost-bitten is Friday, frozen to the core.
I weep this Saturday, forever more.

Is it coincidence that Douglass asked, "What to a slave is the Fourth of
    July?"?
And today I ask what to America is its freedom proclamation?

Again, I am being forthcoming on the Fourth of July.

Can I Hope?

What can hope do for me?
That I can't do for myself?
I have seen the future's eye
I have seen hope

Optimistic am I, but why
When terror lives at my door
Swindled at every corner's ore
I have been hope

Logic tells me, reverse, take cover
The Oracle have told what's to come
But as a fool, I go forward,
Because the end can't come to pass, if it has never begun
Where can I find hope?

We ran on hope, a change in mind
A scene for all, a dark pass behind
Be it creed, politicians' greed, or desperate need
We were a people, we were hope

Feel the sting of a bitter frost
Never mind the generation lost
Frozen soul with shattered heart
Hope some more, a people's part

TERRY LEE WATSON

Filled with pride, I stand
Nothing came from hope
With self-knowledge, I am the now,
The time has come to suspend hope

Finders beware of hope to be found
False hope is a danger, known founders have drowned
Seek truth instead, its depths are unknown
Less have drowned in truth, finder. This has been shown

The Legacy and Legend That Is White Supremacy

I will begin this moment by outlining the most incredible tricks instilled in the legacy of white supremacy to keep this legendary ideology and its institutions alive. Yes, I am using my words carefully.

The most brilliant trick of white supremacy is to convince society that the hue of the skin is directly related to the consciousness of the mind. This grand deception allows for the credo of white supremacy to be transformed and translated with little exertion.

The most remarkable example I can give is when I presented the most common mistakes made in the diversity, equity, and inclusion (DEI) field to a group of police officers. There is a general movement to hire black police officers, and when I ask why, I am typically met with blank stares.

"What do you mean? Shouldn't we want to diversify our police force?"

"Why?" I ask.

I don't ask that because I'm attempting to be difficult; I know that diversifying can be for presentation purposes only. My question is, Are you hiring black officers for presentation or representation reasons? If those black police officers bring with them black culture and black consciousness along with their black skin, how will your current culture react? Will you attempt to celebrate or denigrate their blackness? Or are you looking for (and my friends hate this when I ask this) a Barbie spray-painted brown? Do you hope to show off your new Negro willing to practice, partake, and participate in this legacy? The dark hue of the skin doesn't mean there is a black consciousness within.

White supremacy presents itself in multiple modes and means and therefore never allows itself to be identified or destroyed.

This one might hit home for you, so allow your mind this excursion. If white supremacy were a company, its marketing team would be legendary.

All puns intended. White supremacy has marketed itself as or through religion, patriotism, education, legislation, justice, science, fashion, culture, order, family, and even love. Its flexibility and adaptability to the times allow it to stay alive. By presenting itself in multiple modalities and means, it can ensure it will reach a broad audience no matter its level of comfort.

White supremacy convinces the populace that only white people engage in and with the legacy of white supremacy. Reflecting on the first trick of consciousness, I could not forget the actions that help keep the legend alive. If we can allow our knowledge of existence to be tainted with the legendary legacy of white supremacy, what chances do our efforts and engagement have to avoid this pandemic of epic proportions?

Breathe

Allow me to think like a linguist and explain this truth as I see it. I describe white supremacy as legendary but not because I accept its doctrine or consider it a beneficial contribution to our land. No, the contrary is more the case. I describe white supremacy as legendary because its narrative is rooted in and routed throughout our land, and its great evils have withstood the test of time. From each legend is born a record, and this record is without limits and quite legendary.

A legacy implies the inheritance of something, the passing down of something, and that can include the ignorance that the white supremacy ideology so willingly passes down. However, I tend to look further through its institutions. So I ask whom this inheritance is meant to benefit. As I continue to consider this ideology, I must address what I believe white supremacy to be. But most important, I must address what I think it is not or partially not.

Let's begin with the word *white*. I start here because my experience has shown me that most are hung up on that word and allow the narrative that only white people or white supremacists can participate in the evolution of this legacy. I strongly disagree. If you believe white people are the only or even the primary component of white supremacy, I expect defensiveness or even a wall that would prohibit genuine and honest discussions of this topic. I have concluded this because it tends to result in guilt, anger, and sometimes both in my white supremacy conversations.

However, this is not how I define white supremacy; thus, the two words that make up this ideology—*white* and *supremacy*—must remain a one-word adjective that describes the doctrine and the institutions it maintains. A person might find it difficult to accept this definition because white supremacy usually contains the concept of white people being superior to other races. Though portions of that may be valid, I do not think it defines this legend or legacy well.

A superb example is the idea that a black child can look at a black doll and a white doll and begin to demonize the black doll while glorifying the white doll. If you haven't seen the video, search the internet for "black doll white doll video."

When I talk about the legendary legacy of white supremacy, I am talking about the narrative passed down from generation to generation producing these complexities with self-identity and developing the origins of self-hate. I am talking about the ability to inflict self-hate and in turn self-harm, the ability for a black body to look at another black body and see it as this legacy would have us see us. I am talking about the ability to instill an inferior complex that accepts this perception as accurate. And with this consciousness, we carry this sickness and knowingly pass it down to the next generation.

Minister Malcolm X proposed the question, Who taught you to hate yourself? I ask, Who will teach me to love myself?

At the beginning of this book, I mentioned that unshackling the legacy of white supremacy has been my greatest challenge. Anytime I reflect on a situation, interaction, or thought, I have to see if my reaction is through the lens of white supremacy. If it is, I understand that it has made my black body its ally through its legacy.

I watched the conversation between James Baldwin and Nikki Giovanni in November 1971. Something that James said speaks to this reflection of the legendary legacy of white supremacy. He identified how we as black people take to the word and become collaborators and accomplices in our downfall. We become a part of this legacy that is set on destroying us all.

Breath

I was discussing with someone about a recent attack on an Asian American woman by a black man. The person tried to use this as an example of the angry, out-of-control black man. After listening, I said, "You've fallen for one of the greatest tricks of white supremacy."

In Observation Of ...

My surrounding does not come past me.
On the contrary, I pass through my surrounding
In my passing, I am permitted to observe.

I see ...
Brick building housed with different tribulations,
A grandma raising her granddaughter while her son passes by.
A black mother silently nods while she listens to the blues with a paper
    bag in hand.
An elevator.
A crack bottle.

I smell ...
The cooking from the ancestral spirit, the aroma, is in the air.
The atman of struggle, living, and survival. Of love.
A spirit left out too long, a joint shared among friends.
An intoxicated man who did not make it home,
An elevator.
A crack bottle.

I feel ...
What I am allowed to. The feeling doesn't come naturally.
I am angry my anger is not allowed.
I smile when I am saddened.
I frown when I wonder.
My mind may feel sick, but no time to ponder this; there is so much afoot.
    My empathy is desired. My love is forever welcomed.
But my anguish swings the pendulum, so I am left in observation ...

TERRY LEE WATSON

How Comfortable?

I titled this moment "How Comfortable?"

To my brothers and sisters of all races, creeds, and nationalities,
Of all sexes and orientations,
Of all religions, abilities, and economic status,
Here we are today, together.
As Westerners, we must ask ourselves one honest question: How comfortable
    are we with the legacy of white supremacy?
Do we accept its doctrine, its ways, its security?
Do we worry about what will become of us in its demise?
Are we befriended by it? Do we see it as a charted pathway to prosperity?
Are our dignity and our safety embedded in it? Do we celebrate its triumph?
    What are its victories to us?

Before you can answer these questions, consider that our land has never been without white supremacy and our consciousness never untainted by it. Like the trees, it is instilled in the landscape of America. White supremacy does not cast a shadow, but it is as firm and solid as the land on which we stand on and for, for which people were slaughtered and enslaved on and for. It is our America.

But I am moved by a contradictory doctrine that propelled me to denounce white supremacy today. A celebratory belief that equality shall prevail and that its Colossus shall reign true. One day, we can stop living on a dream and allow our consciousness to come to fruition instead. I denounce white supremacy because I don't need its approval for my conscience, nor do I need its substance or substance abusers. I have my ancestral pride, dignity, and perseverance and therefore do not invite the institution of white supremacy to be introduced. White supremacy fosters lies that produce the foundation on which this institution stands.

I will not be befriended by it, nor will I accept its definition of prosperity. I accept the demise of white supremacy because only then can America meet its obligations under which it was chartered. Only then can equality equate to the promise of the pursuit of happiness. Only then will America let all who breathe partake in its freedoms. White supremacy's demise is critical to the patriotic tenet.

TERRY LEE WATSON

They Called Me N**ger

They called me nigger, but at least they called me at all

All I need is this money, and this respect, and this notoriety.

Notoriety comes at a price, and so does my dwellings

Dwelling on where I came from, who I am, and what is the derivative of my anguish

Anguish so strong, so make it short, let the sting be diminished, but not diminish my being

Being who I am is what I have left, so calling me nigger, is part of the "at least."

They called me nigger because maybe they forgot my name

Name this patriot, this founder, my owner, and I will put you in my portrait's frame

Frame me because you can and privatize my people and me. These prisons exist still?

Still, I remain quiet, solemn internally, but my external must keep this smile for a while.

While I blend, I stay asleep because woke means I can't partake in this fictional cast.

Cast away my sanity; no need for it because they called me nigger, and it is now part of my name.

They call me nigger because this is what has historically been done

Done by promises and dreams, sustained by the continuation of hope

Hope to live life and liberty, freedom is not free, but you have not paid your bill

Bill of rights doesn't seem right to me. Let me read this document of the slaveholder

Holder of my liberty and the disease to my conscience. Let my mind be free

Free from your history, and maybe then I will not be called nigger.

Have You Checked on Your Negro Slave Today?

Boy, he is quiet; all must be well
All must have been forgotten, obliterated hell.
My Negro slave is free, no need to dwell
I have released you from bondage; now you may go.

I abided by my American ideals.
I now must sleep, go, Negro, and heal.
Emancipation is all; freedom was not part of the deal
My Negro is all right; that's what I know.

The science that told me, my Negro had no feelings
Is now responsible for telling me how my Negro feels.
Be grateful, Negro, and be humble in the American dealings.
I am the one, Negro, who let you go.

Your servitude was appreciated.
Time to go, Negro slave
So my consciousness can be alleviated.
Civil without chaos, it's time to pay for freedoms.

"Oh Massa, is not four hundred years of bondage enough?"

Go before I make laws to take you back.
Your bed is still made; it's still warm in your shack.

TERRY LEE WATSON

We Are Sick in Disguise

We are sick in disguise
Our sanity in the demise
So, pray a prayer's prayer

We are long time dying
Forever freedom fighter trying
Pray a prayer's prayer

We are conscious beings
With heart, thoughts, and feelings
So pray a prayer's prayer.

We are the sons of the brightest ray
The daughters of the newest day
Pray a prayer's prayer

We are the past of the forgotten
Uplifted souls in a country's rotten
Pray a prayer's prayer

What I've seen, what I saw
What is left fighting for
Pray a prayer's prayer

We are a strong people, weakened.
We are forever marching mountaintop peaking.
A prayer's prayer is needed.

Reflecting on America's Reaction to the Killing of Ahmaud Arbery (blog post 5/8/2020)

As I prepare to address a university from the Netherlands on the topic of police brutality in America, I glance at the questions they sent me in preparation. The first question they are asking me to address is why police brutality happens and under what conditions and why it continues to occur. I read this question in light of this week's events and the shooting death of Ahmaud Arbery, which has truly shaken me.

Those who shot and killed Mr. Arbery were not active law enforcement; however, according to *USA Today*, Greg McMichael, the father, was a fellow police officer; therefore, Arbery's killers should bear a level of responsibility. Reflecting on this situation, I do not need permission to be angry and distrust a justice system considering the lack of justice. But what gets to me is the feeling that I have seen this behavior represented in America's response before.

When I first read this story about a twenty-five-year-old black man being gunned down in Georgia by Travis McMichael, thirty-four, and his father, Gregory McMichael, sixty-four, I thought, *Here we go again*. As the story developed and with the video's release, it was no surprise to see an outcry for the arrest of the McMichaels. I have come to know this cycle. An incident happens, the evidence is withheld from the public, video and audio evidence is released to the public, public outcry develops, and the presentation of justice pursues. I will classify this as a justice presentation because a trial has not yet taken place and therefore a conviction is not upon us.

However, on May 6, 2020, I came up with a question. With the video's release and the executioner's own recant of what happened, why was there no arrest in February, March, or even April? Seeing a man jogging, pursing him in a truck with a handgun and shotgun, and then killing him sound straightforward. Their story of believing Arbery was involved in burglaries does not clear them of ill intent or justify their approaching him with arms. So I ask still, why no arrest? Why no presumption of wrongdoing? And to answer my question, it's merely the embedded narrative in the fabrication of America.

In 2017, Andre Fede, an author, professor, and lawyer, published *Homicide Justified*,[2] which provides an in-depth comparative look (as stated in its subtitle) into the legality of killing slaves in the United States and the Atlantic world. In this and other books that capture the narratives of slavery in the United States, legal amplifications and progression throughout time are analyzed and the culture and attitudes presented within America too. As this book promises, it respectfully covers the debate among the standards of enslaved homicides throughout time and its societal lack of retribution, and it embarks on the consciousness of the mindset that allows for this debate's existence.

So that leads me to ponder how a man jogging can be murdered in a free society meant to protect all citizens. Even more so, how can this society still lack retribution? First, I believe that reformed laws are without honest intent, which means that the rules at least in America have not been reformed due to moral or religious obligations or due to the consideration of the suffering or generational trauma caused. Its changes are for the benefit of the oppressor, not the oppressed. The progression of reformed rules occurred only with the promise to continue the legacy and the cognition of white supremacy. This is how a district attorney, a police force, and yes, the murderers themselves could sleep at night for nearly two months. Woven in their cognition from centuries of narratives, Arbery must have been guilty because he fit a description.

The false narratives that allowed a free society to have slaves and

---

[2] Andrew T. Fede, *Homicide Justified: The Legality of Killing Slaves in the United States and the Atlantic World*. University of Georgia Press, 2017. Project MUSE muse.jhu. edu/book/52491.

murder them exist today. While the institution of slavery in American transformed, the mindset, social cognition, the thriving will of white supremacy are as well as they have ever been.

I want to address the title "The Evolution of Master-Slave Killing." To deal with healing, we have to acknowledge the wounds in the first place. I am afraid that still, in America, we lack the understanding of the development of our country's consciousness. We are projected to repeat ourselves tragedy after tragedy because we refuse to face our past and its hypocrisies.

The Mass Lynching of the Conscious Mind

Dear politician, you are a product of white supremacy in America.

The eyes you use to smile on the campaign trail smiled behind the hood or in blackface.

The hand you use to shake the hand of the black man is the same hand you use to press your white robes, the same hand that applied the greasepaint.

I hold no sorrow for this photo as it is what I expect. No shock. No surprise.

I had a thought that I thought I would share tonight. This habitual contemplation has found its way across my mind quite often. The question is, What has changed? Now I know that question is loaded and without direction can be interpreted differently. But for me, it always renders the asking but without the expectation of an answer. Well, until now.

I titled this moment "The Mass Lynching of the Conscious Mind." For a minute or two, as black people, we allowed ourselves to believe the American mind held goodwill toward us. It saw us as a constituent of the national party, and we black people would be welcome as any other partygoer. This is truly a lynching of our conscience. With all the evidence and history that our land has afforded us, we still believe. I still believed.

I talk about liberation and freedom a lot. Even in this collection of moments, you will hear me refer to liberation and freedom as the goal— freedom of body, the liberation of the mind, the freedom to be. But what I failed to talk about until now was what constituted this level of emancipation. Well, I find two notions have been part of this narrative. One "I take" vs. "They have given me" my freedom/liberation.

If It Is Not My Home

I have been told that my country is my home as well as yours. I was led to believe that we are neighbors and brethren. If I believe this to be true, peace is what I expect when I am around you.

If you were to invite me into your space, I would assume that you would extend with it your greatest hospitality as I would if I were to extend an invitation to you. I would want you to feel right at home in my home. I would ask if you were thirsty, and no beverage I had would be off limits. I would ask if you were hungry, and my courtesy would extend just so.

When you are invited into someone's home, there should be no assumption that your comfort equals theirs. If the home is too cool for your liking, you would not assume that your perception is congruent.

I record these expectations on home and hospitality with meaning.

So why does my country not feel like my home? Why must I wait for the rules of hospitality to apply in my own home? The concept of brethren should not be so shadow' and its reality should be as solid as steel. I am no longer looking for hospitality in my home because my ancestors paid that bill. The water and the food that this home holds belongs to me also.

Silence Is Believing

Through jokes and seldom attacks
No one speaks
In violation of my god given rights
No one speaks

When pain is sure to come
No one speaks
They call themselves the children of Israel
But remain silent, mild, and meek

When the crowd disrupts my peace
Did you think to speak?
Did you see me as an outsider?
Did you not call me brother?

Virtual in my mind, so I can't be quiet
Mellow be my soul, left to ponder loss of humanity
Speak, your silence is eroding the soul
Speak, your silence says more then you know

If you call yourself a child of light
If the chaos speaks to you, will you take flight
Speak
Speak
Sp ... ...

Died Once, Died Twice, Died Three Times

Thus far, I have considered myself in control of my emotions. Well, until now. I felt this moment titled "Died Once, Died Twice, Died Three Times."

It is fitting that I end the American celebration with this moment. It comes as no surprise that I find myself silent and listening to others verbalize what they believe is factual because that is what I tend to do. I have always tried to understand before being understood, but from time to time, I come across people who willingly show me that they may be unable to reason. It is this that allows me to end with the following.

Died Once

It is an internal struggle to want to partake in a dream that was not dreamed for us. This internal struggle comes with pressure and guilt, love and despair, and each day, I find myself asking if this is what I really want. Do I continue to strive for a reality that is not real or create a universe as I see fit? What does that look like? Where do I start? Who is a part of it?

Died Twice

I am doomed to struggle externally finding myself forever on the outside of the American bubble looking through it. I can see the other side, but do I go through or around the bubble to get to my destination? To go through the bubble means that I have decided to strive for a reality that has not yet been real and allow opportunities to heal my sick mind pass by. If I choose to go around it, have I given up on the American dream? I am left to defend my thoughts, my actions, and my right to freedom not only from those who seek to oppress but also from those who are oppressed. It is difficult to show you, world, that your mind is just as tainted as mine is.

Died Three Times

Keeping me from this American celebration is America's pastime. A dysfunctional family that refuses to go to counseling because they are afraid of being stigmatized. Knowing what is right and how to achieve good but consistently selecting what is easy and what is nice. Demonizing the struggler but not the cause of the struggle.

What is there worth fighting for?

CHAPTER 3
I FIGHT FOR
MY PEOPLE

Have you ever heard someone use the phrase "Speak truth to power"? The phrase *truth to power* got me thinking—Whose truth? And empowering whom? Let me open up this collection of fighter's moments with an understanding.

Fighter's Heart

I admire those who take a stand against the legacy of white supremacy. It takes heart to take on something that has been so stagnant. Heart! It also reminds me of an article I read about Dr. Martin Luther King Jr.'s heart.

He was assassinated at age thirty-nine. However, the autopsy revealed that he had a heart of a nearly sixty-year-old man. The doctors believe this was due to the constant stress he was under. To give our hearts for our people is unfathomable yet expected in the land that sustains the evilness of racism and bigotry. So to the fighter's heart, we must understand the toll it takes on a person, a body, and a mind.

Fighter's Mind

It is with this view of the heart that I now pay homage to the fighter's mind. I spend an ordeal talking about a sick mind and with great reason. In the mind of a fighter, he must always be three steps ahead. He must know not only what his move will be but also anticipate the moment of hate and animosity and more important, how his actions will follow.

After giving a speech, I was asked how I prepared for my lectures. Of course I practice, make sure my talking points flow, and do something that I encourage anyone with a fighter's mind to do—I read the news and the opinion column. I look for the opinions I heartily disagree with, and I write a response I save for the keeper's sake. I do this because I know that when I set out to challenge a legacy as sturdy as white supremacy, I will be met with its defenders looking to sustain its heritage. To me, remaining astute is not just wise; it also helps maintain the spirit.

Fighter's Spirit

"I fight for my people," a retired marine once told me. I tend to speak to not only my friends, family, and associates about deconstructing racism head-on but also to strangers. This warm fall Alabama day, I talked to this retired marine. I asked him a question I typically do not ask because I deem it disrespectful, but for some reason, I asked it anyway: "As a black man, why did you decide to serve?"

To add some context to this conversation, I was walking through the lynching memorial in Montgomery, Alabama, something every American should do, and came across this individual. He told me about his grandfather who had served and how badly he had been treated when he returned. The story of his grandfather reminded me of the group the Harlem Hell Fighters. This all-black regiment fought in World War I to return home to a Jim Crow country filled with hate and lynchings. This marine shared how fortunate he was to have had this relationship with his grandfather and to remember the stories and how they impacted him as an adult. I thought, *Does this mean you entered service knowing what your granddaddy went through? Why?* So that is when I asked that question.

Well, as he said, "I fight for my people."

There is no spirit more extraordinary than that of a fighter with a cause. The trick to me is to identify that cause to maintain that spirit, to acknowledge how the spirit may be strong but can send a heart and a mind to their demise.

Recognize fighters for who they are, people who have accepted strained hearts, sick minds, and weary spirits for their people.

My Pride's Domicile

It is with a new level of criticism that I write this. I resent fear and anger, and I must sustain my optimism for a fighter's sake. The importance of this is even greater now than ever. The warriors of hate are around waiting to see if I will allow my fighter's cause to drown. They should know I am regal and royal, always carry my crown, and never let acts of hatred bring me down.

My pride is alert, and it tells me that everything and nothing is worth fighting for, dying for. My pride tells me that no one can give me something I cannot take for myself. This mindset is as liberating as it gets. To feel I have what it takes to identify truth, look it in the face, and say, "Now I am stronger," gives me ... well, pride.

I tell people that the best thing they can do for the liberation cause is to understand the difference between the champion, the player, and the fan. The champion is one who by choice wearies under the burden. When times are rough, people look to the champion to weather the storm and come out of it better. The player on the other hand is in the game with the champion. He wears the same uniform and know the same plays but is not looked at when climbing the horizon gets tough. The player is not criticized as harshly if things don't go according to plan. Although he has a responsibility and a role, no one consistently focuses on him.

Now the fan. He can cheer on and support the champion and the player or scold them when things are rough. He can act as if he were never with the champion and player at the turn of a hat.

Who are you? Where does your pride reside? Are you proud to be a fan, a nonparticipatory ally waiting to see how the team does? Waiting for the right moment to make a call on your allegiance? Identifying what the other fans are doing? Do you stay to the last minute during challenging times or leave to find the place that gives you comfort? Is this your pride's domicile?

Are you a player willing to learn the game's plays, benefit from the rewards, and avoid the criticism of a downfall? Are you here to give it your all only when you are called on but silently going through the motions saving face and place? Where does your pride reside?

Are you a champion fighting tooth and nail every moment of every play because you have chosen to take on this burden? To take on the responsibility of being ridiculed and ostracized by the fan who once support you if you happen to no longer show him what he expects to see from a champion? Without acknowledging the heart, mind, or spirit that you have given them thus far?

Where does my pride domicile?

Sick Mind of America

Sick mind of America.

What makes your mind so sick?

Quick to judge my downfalls, quick to judge, yet your morality is
counterfeit.

Is it the complexities of the consciousness?

A broken bound, mental enslavement.

Brought upon me from broken bodies on slaves' ships?

Sick mind of America.

Is not your sane mind well?

Flustered with lies of portrayed portraits.

Broken spirits in rusted cells.

This truth is true truth.

So you do best to know it as well.

Sick mind of America.

What be your purpose? Have you not sought peace or refuge? Do you deny
the symptoms and the cause of infliction?

Stay sick, because being well may also bring redemption.

I once was sick with you. This is easy to do when your sickness is contagious.

If Jesus wept, why shouldn't I?

Why don't you?

Sick mind of America.

Have we lost our way? Has our path to righteousness's sake been blocked,
its bridge collapsed?

This Land Does Not Deserve a King

I struggled with this title for some time, but I am sure now that it is correct. I speak to this land from within this land. Therefore, I speak from within my rights. I write this on the eve of Martin Luther King Jr.'s birthday. I believe this land, America, does not deserve a king or a savior. This land has chosen its path, and its path is not one of peace, justice, or equality. Its roads and paths are painted golden with greed, and its earthy soil is fertile with oppressed blood and tears.

This land does not deserve a king.

Laughter may come but only after tears. Love may come but only after hate. This land has made it clear that you cannot have one without the other, and for some, the other may never come. 'Merica, dare to praise a king and impair a prince and defile its queen. So my words of not deserving a king are valid. This king stood for peace and prosperity for all, and this land stands for war and prosperity for some.

Each year, a land pays tribute to its king yet neglects his proclamations, all he stood for, and most important, it shows little interest in moving on the path in which his movement was known.

TERRY LEE WATSON

America Is Not the Land It Has Been Doctrined to Be

America is not the land that it has been doctrined to be.

This condition has always been plain and clear to me.
Home of the free, yet freedoms denied, America lost its identity and pride?
No, Its obstacles too great, its sins too deep.
America portrays the lion, the lamb, and the sheep.
Its identity is false, its pride is veined, no love is sought, no knowledge is
    gained.

America is not the land that it has been doctrine to be.

It lies about its freedoms, the liberty contract is not legit.
I thought it doctrine was true, must not have read the fine print.
Or maybe it's written in the soil with the sweat of its laborers.
Maybe it's written on the tree roots in Georgia, with the blood of Mary
    Turner and her baby.
My unrecognizable consciousness leaves me alone among the masses
I'm okay with this because it is my fruit to bear ...

America is not the land that it has been doctrine to be.

This is not a doctrine of unpatriotic proportions.

At the Hand of Injustice

If I died by the hands of injustice, what will be my story?

Would it be perpetuated by a stereotype, lined with reason or "said truth?"

Or will it speak of the injustice and need for change?

Will I be a hashtag? Will I be remembered? And will those who call me friend speak my name?

Or would my suffix be change to "thug" or "criminal" or culturally insane?

If I died by the hands of injustice, what will you say about me?

Will I be a good father, a good husband, or a man?

Not afraid to speak up, or fight, or take a stand.

Or will my stature be combined with those I don't know?

Will you tell them about me, or will you let them tell you who I was?

If I died by the hand of injustice, what would become of my family!

Would my father be the cause, or would he be a man who lost a son?

Would my kids be pitied, or would their suffering be consoled by the statistics?

Will you speak of unwed mothers, and lost fathers, or the homes without peace?

Or will pray for my widow, speak in your churches, your communities, and your streets?

If I died by the hand of injustice, how will you remember me?

A friend, a foe, or maybe someone you really didn't know?

Will you unfriend me, unfollow me, deny my intent?

Speak from the heart because the heart is *known* not to vent?

Or would you take the painful journey to redefine your truth?

Come to the conclusion that there is truth that lies beyond you?

Would you feel pain, pity, or sorrow?

Will you tell yourself "No one is promised tomorrow"?

Or will you work to redefine the promise of tomorrow?

Work through the pain, pity, and sorrow, and rise to tell your family and
    friends that I was not your enemy but that I was tomorrow.

If I died by the hands of injustice, will justice be found?

Will someone speak of the injustice as if it were never around?

Will you listen and say, "The light will end the darkness" or "Truth shall
    be found"?

Even if the only light that holds the truth is in the hands of the injustice
    right now?

What would be my headline? What will be shared?

Will it speak of my great doings or moments of despair?

Would it paint a picture? Or reflect as a mirror?

Will it work to separate or bring people closer together?

Would it do as I like or do as you like?

Will this art be diminished by signs that say "Fight"?

Who would change truth, speak the story of the untold?

Will you share the moments we broke bread, or will you throw stones?

Who would you change? What would you say?

Change: Would you start with yourself? Would you say what I've said?

I once spoke these words when I spoke to black youth ... I said,

"If we were all created equal, then why do we think so differently?

If a man is our brother, then why we treat them like our foes?

We may not change today or tomorrow, but we can always change how we
    think about each other and how we treat each other."

Would you speak?

If I died by the hand of injustice, would it be in vain?

Would you be overcome by angry thoughts and pain?

Change the truth! That is what I want you to do.

Change the truth! Without anger or pain.

Without vengeance, without judgment, without denying my name.

Statistics! Don't need them

Media! Don't want them

It cannot tell my truth! My truth is an untold story known to none except you!

If I died by the hands of injustice but known that my truth may have influenced you,

I die happy because my justice may be found through you.

You can speak of my peace, of my wife, of my kids,

You can speak of the world, in which I once lived.

How we were not equals, we may not have thought the same,

But my life has influenced you all the same.

You will speak of me, of who I was, and what I would do,

Not as an outlier or the exception to the rule.

You may speak of my truth and how it is not parallel to your truth,

But a truth nevertheless, a truth. That is what I would want you to do!

You can call my kids and tell them what a good man I was,

Not forget them, because that's what they need,

Trust me, if injustice had its way, they would want my kids to bleed.

Not to see their truth, or value who I was

But to prepare for the inevitable because that is what injustice does.

You can stand against injustice because you too have a light,

And with that light you can shred darkness and watch those around you take flight.

It is not easy to be a light holder for injustice targets them too,

But you will be strong because that is what I want you to do.

So if I were to die by the hands of injustice,

I hope it was with great reason.

Breaking Bondage

My naked soul as it is, it needs no explaining
Your skin is your beauty, my child, no complaining
Purposed by the creator, I am not for sale
Speak loudly, speak well, you are not for sale

A slave is man-made, but a man's choice is projection
Let not the mind be chained, yet let it reach for perfection

In bondage we sing, in freedom we scream
In bondage we march, in freedom we stomp
The oppressor can't tell the oppressed how to deal with oppression
My voice won't be silent. This is my true confession

Painstaking this journey may be, but it's worth the taking
A history untold is a future unknown, a decedent left forsaken

Spirit be led, no conscious be bound
Who among the lion pride be found?

I, saith I, a child in a mature world
I, saith, I, either it be boy or girl
I, saith, I, a purpose with complexity
Love and kindness are weak, without authenticity

Break from it
Break from it
And don't turn back
Yearn to learn from it
So we don't go back

Preach

Black man, stand. Don't take a stand
Black man, breathe, "Fuck your breath"
Drop what's not there and raise your hands
Preach!

Black lady, walk, don't walk away from me
Black lady, quiet, "Answer me when I speak"
Bend unnaturally in this direction but don't you reach
Preach!

Black boy, be still, don't you move
Black boy, stay home, "Find comfort in this cell"
I got my eyes on you and stay calm
Preach!

Black girl, stay, don't except your beauty
Black girl, live, your body but my choice
Black girl, watch your black mamma
Preach!

TERRY LEE WATSON

Why Kaepernick Sat

The country wants a party while justice remains divisible
I find no truth in power, but the power of truth is overbearing
Burnt houses of prayer, blood soaks the pulpit
Though all of its injustice, America sits?

So, I stand with Kap, as he sat

Or as he takes a knee, you feel like that's un-American
And not when Crawford in an open-carry state bleeds?
Our soldiers come home, and we can't find the money to house them
We use them for photo ops and ignore the demons that surround them

So, I stand with Kap, as he sat

Or as Black Lives Matter lied down, a slave set free
Yet denied his liberty. From Freedom Bureau Act
Our country doesn't know how to act. 'Tis sweet land is propaganda
So we stay comfortable with propaganda until we elect the Republican
    once a Democrat

So, I stand with Kap, as he sat,

So that lady's liberty light stays lit
its leadership remains constitutionally unfit
Bound by it constitutes, in order to replace the new Colossus,

The home of the free, never free, and the brave, abandoned and forgotten. If this land is noble and free, then sip the water from Flint, MI, please.

So, I stand with Kap, as he sat,

And you would too if you hold the patriotic symbol accountable and true.

TERRY LEE WATSON

Nuts and Bolts

Upon my emancipation, Massa said,

"Pull yourself up by your bootstraps and walk a straight line

A line so defined by America's pride."

(New to this American celebration, who am I to decline?)

"Don't be a victim," Massa told me. "Behold the land of milk and honey."

"Should you ever dream and fantasize of such a great space," Massa warned,
    "Just remember to stay in your place."

"I am the machine, and you, you are just the loose nuts and bolts," Massa
    reminded me.

"I am not the one who runs this country, boy. I am just the design for your
    refinement. But one day soon might be your time."

I felt like I was having thoughts for the first time.

A capsule was collected, and my consciousness detected

"Your mind is young, but soon it may be perfected," Massa told me.

"So, when the time shall come, you will be like me. But for now,

I am the machine and you, you are just the loose nuts and bolts."

Massa was trying to tell me that I may have this oil from his second drip
    pan and experience the joy.

"I am a man, your leader, and you are just a boy."

I thought, and I responded.

"Massa, can a machine run without nuts and bolts either attached or not?

Can a machine function or be proper without such parts? No, I say it can't."

Blink

Please allow me this moment to reassemble my sanity, to readjust my
mind. Have you ever pondered the characteristics of those who fight for
a just cause and those who fight—just cause? Let's take our topic, racism.

Think about those who fight against racism and those who just fight allowing racism to be one of their confrontations.

I imagine the moment when a fighter finds the courage to fight for a reason and forgoes any obstacles that kept them from the fight. Where does it come from? Was the will to fight always there deep in its domain waiting for the chance to be free? What does that sound like, feel like?

I came across an activist who had a fighter's cause and with it a way of interpreting success and a method of constructing a pathway to a warrior's mission. But I also know many among us who fight just causes. The fight is what moves these warriors, not the causes. The action is what sustains them. Not the progression toward goals. Goals aren't necessary. This presents a conflict between two mindsets over time and becomes a battle between warriors. The mind of a massa letting go and of a slave learning of his freedom.

But what can we learn from both minds to help us deconstruct white supremacy? First, be careful of whom you gain your fighter's fuel from. You might be surprised that we sometimes depend on the fight to get our fuel and not the progression proving that we are loose nuts and bolts. Be fine-tuned to the goal you seek. Let progression be your refill.

Second, consider where your vehicle is traveling and how many pit stops you can afford. I found myself in far too many situations that prompted me to ask myself, *Is this worth my time?* It's a waste of energy to use it up without progress or without learning.

Who decides where you go? Is it your oppressor or your newfound free consciousness? I often take time out to make sure that the people around me in this fight are there for the cause and not just cause. Take time to tighten your nuts and bolts.

Infringed

Slaughtered shadows of the pass leave an imprint
Fellow man where once I stood leaves a footprint
If time is what we need to wash away our deeds
Then the deeds are not meant to be taken away

Infringed

Shallow soul left seeking a space, a place in time
Living life to the greatest, breathing is divine
Thoughts without action remain unknown
Actions without thoughts leave us alone

Infringed

Burden beings leaving strengthens wills
Persistence is gained, its historic chills
Signed my sanity, my mind seen plenty
Taught with truth and touched with love

Infringed

Pardon my party; it knows I'm not well
But it tells of my hopes, but my hopes never tell
My identity remains constant, but my thoughts may change
My reality is less real, my reality is stained

Infringed

A law written for "we," but "I" am invisible
Emancipation is "free," yet my proclamation remains divisible.
Long lived this fright, chained to a wall no lesser are we
A man, or three-fifths. Take a stand and speak of your freedom

Infringed

TERRY LEE WATSON

Evil Beholds Me

I don't mind the evil as long as I am comfortable
As long as my sleep is not disturbed and my dreams remain intact

I don't mind the evil as long as it doesn't penetrate my bubble
And allow my atmospheric orb to be compromised and tainted

I don't mind the evil and myself can be changed
As long as I can prosper in this iniquitous land and smile

My child's conscious is not for their own
I will make them okay with evil too

If they learn to expect the evil now, maybe its sting will be lessened
Don't be yourself or your best; this land is wicked, and demon infested

Eventually, they will accept you if you don't mind
Behold the evil through space and time

Don't mind it, not one little bit
It roots are entangled in this lion's pit

The Antiracist and the Reformed White Supremacist

What separates an activist from an average Joe? An activist is never satisfied while the average Joe remains content. Remember what I said during the walk?

I had the opportunity to speak to two individuals—one who saw himself as antiracist and the other who described himself as a reformed white supremacist. What stood out to me in this communication with these two was not just their passion for eradicating the hate of racism but also their methods of doing so.

I thought this would be the perfect time to revisit this moment under the section "I Fight for My People." Please do not misunderstand me or my perception regarding antiracism. This movement of not being racist is not enough. It speaks to the undoing of generational trauma. I, however, would like to speak to the similarities and the distinctions of the antiracist and the reformed white supremacist.

The Similarities

As I mentioned, both of these individuals are passionate about individually and systemically eradicating the evils of racism. Both are white and utilize the power of education to help people unlearn what they have learned about racism in our society. I look at both individuals as people with whom I can hold honest conversations about race, and even with their strong wills and fighters' cause, I can see levels of vulnerability. The passion displayed by these two comes from their wanting to undo the harm and establish healing. Both receive death threats and have accepted that their cause comes at a price. That is the spirit of a fighter.

The Distinctions

As far as what makes them different, it is not difficult to describe. Antiracists like to address systemic change and willingly help change others. On the other hand, because of their contributions to the hate, reformed white supremacists feel an urgency to change others and willfully accept addressing the systemic changes as needed.

The guilt that comes from racism is placed differently. Antiracists, because they are unable or unwilling to put themselves as people who cause or caused harm, put the guilt on the system. The placement of the blame is quite the reciprocal for reformed white supremacists. But the most distinct difference between the two can be given from the conversation I had with them directly. When I spoke with the antiracist, he shared many things that I, a black man, could contribute to the fighters' cause, a list of takeaways if you will. However, when I spoke to the reformed white supremacist, he would not accept my help, the reason being, and I quote, "I've done harm to black people. I don't want to burden black people for undoing my harm."

Take from this moment what you will. I leave it thinking about the importance of recognizing where guilt is placed and who remains responsible for undoing the harm of white supremacy.

I Can't Afford to Be Tired

It is 2:00 a.m., and I'm adding the finishing touches to a Juneteenth event I am preparing for. My friend Leslie Laing and I review the last part of our script at that hour all because it has been a long year (2020) and we wanted to make sure our community recognized the importance of this liberation celebration. After I am done and we log off, I decided to write this poem appropriately titled "I Can't Afford to Be Tired."

I am the capturer of narratives and the teller of the stories,
Therefore, I strive to be a beacon of truth.
One of the most approachable questions I get consistently is, "Where do you find the time?"
I am constantly and consistently seeking liberation for all. But I am not alone in this quest, nor is this quest original. Therefore, I call this moment, "I can't afford to be tired."
I can't afford to be tired. Me? No, not I.
Who am I to say I am tired? When I know the struggle is at its beginning. When I know my current being is due to the sacrifices my father made to reject the ideology of tiredness himself.
I can't afford to be tired. Me? No, not I.
What is afforded to me, a tired body? With the knowledge of my ancestor's will. I feel like it is an insult to their memory if I announce tiredness as my weak point, never allowing this wound to heal.
What is tiredness to me but another emotion stored and embodied in the perseverance of my fighter's cause. Tiredness is not in the march but in the mind that continues to ponder.
I can't afford to be tired. No, I can't.
This God has not given to me. A gift or curse of hope, a gift or curse it'll be.
I can't afford this notion, never. I now have a generation to consider, bitter, might that taste be, I cannot wilt or wither.

If ever allowed my eyes to close, what thoughts will be allowed to run? If
ever allowed to rest at will, no, not until my last breath is done.

I can't afford to be tired. No, I can't.

Injustice I learn takes no breaks, so therefore neither do I. I may weep your
pain but never allowing my soul to cry.

Help!

It is not a word reserved for all,

Help!

It is not the world that I loathe or adore.

I can't afford to be tired. Me? No, not I.

Oppression sees my tiredness as a weak point; I see it as the peak of my
endurance will.

Energized by my ancestral wisdom, water, earth, fire, wind, be still.

Kill these thoughts of inferiority.

Kill these notions of inequity.

My being produces only a notion of justice

Freedom is all I will except as a part of this so-called democracy.

Oh, I can't afford to be tired. Me? No, not I.

I feel the pressure come on in the sense of my firstborn son.

So know this fire burning is not at its end. No, my people, this fire has
just begun.

Have Joy and Be Wise

This night was fantastic. I got to listen to two individuals I admire in all senses of the word—Dr. Joy DeGruy and Mr. Tim Wise. The message was powerful, and the discussion about the multigenerational trauma resonated with me. In this discussion, they highlighted one significant challenge they face —convincing America that whiteness exists. As I took in what they were saying, a story resurfaced in my mind.

As a boy, I spent a lot of time by myself, and I liked that. As you know already, I had an odd collection and was a boy who did a lot of thinking. The projects made it so that being outside was not always possible, and because of that, friends were few and far between. I remember taking the graffitied A train to Far Rockaway and being in awe of the shopping strip. But the one thing that always interested me was the people I encountered. As a nine-year-old, I always wondered about the origins of this community.

In the eighties, I remember the old folks always talking about how nice it used to be and how they could leave their doors open without fear of being harmed or bothered. Everyone was a friendly neighbor. I remember the old woman who lived upstairs who made the most intoxicating rum cake. No lie. My mother told me not to eat it because she said it would make me drunk. I didn't believe her, and I tried some anyway.

My mother's best friend, who had a daughter my age, used to drink Old E out of a paper bag as she listened to the blues. She was the only person I knew who made burgers in the oven, which made them bland and dry. She'd sip from her paper bag, close her eyes, and nod to the music. As a child, I never understood why she kept the can in the bag in her own home. That made sense if you were outside, but in your own home? Nope.

I remember all these things, all these people, and I remember how ashamed they were of their youth. They would talk about our generation as if we were lost without a cause. This new hip-hop, this crack, this gold. Never to be associated with "them." They would talk about their sons and their daughters and the evils they committed. They would watch the news and see black boys being shoved into cop cars. These folks would shake their heads and say, "It's a damn shame." They would blame crack for destroying the community and the new generation. Well, it was hopeless. I think Clinton would describe it as super predators.

But at the same time, they would talk about white folks differently— how proper they were, how well they lived. "White folks wouldn't allow this junk in their communities." Sometimes, I would overhear them plan their escape. "If I won the lottery, I'd leave the projects and live in a nice house in a white neighborhood." Even as a boy, this was a great contradiction to my conscience. I was young and didn't have the knowledge I possess today. I did not know about the legacy and characteristics of white supremacy.

So as I sat listening to this scholarly discussion, I was taken back to that time when I was surrounded by my people, black people, as they too held whiteness up on a pedestal, breaking not the chain that bound us mentally but strengthening it. The adults around us mortgaged our minds and deposited our sickness in the escrow of slavery. So I title this moment "Have Joy and Be Wise."

Be still, people, my people. Take pride in your house.
Take peace to the place you dwell, and let it bring you joy, much joy.
Be genuine, people, my people. Revisit your space of contentment.
Allow your space to be your own and own the ambiance that's there still.

Be courageous, people, my people. Take with you your armor if you will.
Be where you are, and where you are, remain peaceful still,
But yet be wise, know what you say; we are listening,
What you are doing, we are watching ready to pass on what you leave us.

Who Is Willing to Carry On?

I have found vulnerability to be a powerful thing. The freedom to proclaim for yourself mental relief is empowering. Let's get vulnerable. Write down your biggest fear. The first time I did this exercise, I put down something I didn't want to happen to my kids or loved ones, a fear that something terrible beyond my control. But then I allowed myself to think beyond that, and what I came up with was more faithful to myself, true to myself, because I may or may not have control of this, but it is worth mentioning.

I love the word *activism*. With every fight, there is a fighter. For every fighter, there must be a person willing to carry on when the fighter can no longer go on. So my biggest fear is that before I leave this world, I will not prepare the generation to do what is necessary to carry on this fight against racism.

Whether it is inability or unwillingness, it haunts me daily. After Martin was assassinated, Coretta carried the torch. After Malcolm was assassinated, Betty carried the torch. So I named this moment "Who Is Willing to Carry On?"

From now to then, from here to there, who is willing to carry on?
What can I give you now to help you find this burden bearable?
Its worthiness? Is it cause? Identifying what is worth fighting for?
Who among you is willing to carry on?
People will see you along the way, so make sure they see your strength.
Bend for no will and nobody. For what you carry is a generation's will to
    carry on themselves.
Pay respect for those who have carried before you. Know them well, your
    predecessors. Learn from them what is right and easy, and may your
    new mind guide you well.
As Langston says, "Hold on to your dreams."
May they take you where you want to go.

Pick your battles, know yourself, and where you need to be, and when.
Choose wisely your players and know where they stand.
And like DMX reminded us, "Always trust everyone to be themselves. But
    trust in the fact you can see them well."
Among them all, know the person who is willing to carry on.

CHAPTER 4
PLAYING THE FIFTH NOTE

THE PLAYING OF THE FIFTH NOTE

By Terry Watson

"Truth takes time and effort. Most people seem to be short of both." A friend posted that on social media. It's true. Time is something we must work to find, and effort is something we must work to maintain.

I have always been fascinated with the relationship between darkness and light. At one point, I thought that both must be present and relevant for either to exist. Without darkness, there could be no light. I however have found a new respect for the relationship between darkness and light. Darkness allows me to appreciate how relevant light is.

This definitive collection of moments describes my reflection of time and effort, one of the greatest struggles of all time. Time and effort. Conversations take time, and understanding takes effort. My reactions and emotions take time and effort to process and internalize, and of course my reflections is not an exception to this conceptualization of thought. Therefore, I am careful to take the time to identify my fifth note. I will talk about the fifth note soon, but for now, remember these four main points.

#organize #strategize #mobilize #materialize

For these last set of moments, consider why it is vital to a sick mind to know when the end is near. As I mentioned initially, even sane, reasonable minds get sick once in a while. The trick is how to make this sick mind well and give it the remedy so it doesn't get sick in the same way again.

A while ago, I was in conversation with a group; the topic was racism at the height of the Trump presidency. I listened, and then I asked, "What in America has changed?"

"People are more comfortable with their racism," someone said.

"To you," I said. I got strange looks. "To you. People are more comfortable with their racism to you." I explained that people's comfort with racism or white supremacy didn't change. It may have changed just around them.

I never want to entertain the idea that racism is a one-directional, one-paradigm outcome. My sick mind permitted that before, and it has caused me nothing but trauma and pain. Thinking that white supremacy was exclusive to some allowed my inability to see its legacy, its hold over America's consciousness, precisely what its legacy is meant to do. Quite legendary indeed.

"To you. People are more comfortable with their racism to you. To me, if they know me, they know where I stand. They know what I will allow and what will cause friction." In other words, they know my fighter's cause because I know my fifth note. And my fifth note, I play it well.

TERRY LEE WATSON

The Unveiling of a Black Man's Eyes

My eyes have seen the glory of the coming of the lord,
yet you can't see my glory because your lord has hidden my eyes.
My eyes have seen the pain and shed a tear for those in grief,
yet you can't see my pain because my grief shall conceal my eyes.

My eyes have seen my people's courage and love,
yet you can't see this beauty because your hate hid my eyes.
My eyes have seen the tribulations and the tranquility within the soul,
yet you can't see these trials because our conflict will hide my eyes.

At this moment, titled "The Unveiling of a Black Man's Eyes," watching the video from 1960 of a black man and his white servant, allows me to reflect on something I hope others will reflect on. The complexity of this moment can be described only with the story I am about to share.

I want you to understand the intimacy that has been taught to me regarding a man's eyes. As were most people I know, I was told very early on to look people in the eyes when I spoke with them as a sign of respect. Avoiding eye contact meant you were lying, being unfaithful, or in some cases terrified. I have committed my truths to this, and even though I generally find eye contact difficult, I wanted to make sure I showed respect.

As I got older, I was told that eye contact not only held this intimate component but also showed your ability to hold your own. I was taught that when you communicated with someone, you showed honesty and strength when you looked them in the eye.

Blink

A man, a product of the help, knows the rules. Do not enter through the front door, always the side. Be quiet. Don't go upstairs. Do not be seen. Speak only when spoken to. Help if you can.

A man removed from the help lifestyle for over a decade pulls up to a spectacular house he visited throughout his childhood. This time, however, this young man has a son, a toddler. Willing to pass on the rules of the help, allowing the inheritance of this sickness to be passed down to his son, a son that believes he is free, this man makes his way to the back door. In a blink of an eye, his son does what a free body does and runs to the front door and rings the bell smiling and waiting to be welcomed in. This young man freezes and hides his eyes.

A young man rushes to the front door and says to his boy, "No, no, no, we have to … No, son, we don't have to. We can stay right here."

Let them see our eyes.

Am I Too, Brute?

"He is." "She was." How can I define someone's character? "I am." "I was." Will I allow someone to explain my own?

I am beginning to think we are meant to see our stories on replay allowing our fear of no one left to carry on come to fruition. Especially when we cannot intervene or engage. Every day and every situation seems like a test of one's being otherwise known as a character check.

How does one character form a decision, or is it the decisions that create our character?

Land of the free, shit. I have let that one go, but does that mean I have lost trust or hope? I find myself asking through moments of wellness, "Am I too, Brute?" From a Shakespearean epilogue, am I my worst enemy and therefore have befriended my foe?

Blink

Am I too, Brute?

Am I content with anger and unable to recognize love? I am left to critique myself, my relationship with my people. When I criticize my own, I might at the same time give a stranger or a foe a pass. I may damn the oppressed and at the same time praise the oppressor.

So am I too, Brute?

I call for my sanity to be unyielding and do not allow myself to think in such a manner. But I am afraid my mind is sick, genuinely unwell. My sense is unyielding only to a mind that consciously turns itself against its own people and allows for mockery and degradation, for the confirmation of despotism partaking from it the devouring of strange fruit from a poplar tree.

This is what I can't do. This is what I must not become. Am I too, Brute? The question that digs at my self-reflecting/projecting identity.

I wonder what my soul has become. Am I the face of my people, or do I deface my people? Do I report that everything is okay in a burning building? Oh sick mind, what shall I do?

Am I too, Brute?

Don't let me be the supplier of the poison when my best interest is better suited as the antidote. Lord, I do not wish to be a detriment to a sane mind anymore. I must be willing to forgo all that makes me a Brute, a Judas kissing salvation goodbye.

TERRY LEE WATSON

A Curse to Know

My country refuses to heal
Requiring broken bodies to kneel
Beware weary minds through troubled times

Knowledge, although good in nature, can impair exploration especially of complex and challenging topics such as racism and white supremacy. Social psychologists have a term for it—the curse of knowledge. If you know it, why would you need to explore it further?

This is one reason people have a tough time talking about ways to progress to the demise of white supremacy. Throughout their lives, they have collected experiences and conformed to their theories of racism and the legacy of white supremacy, which they are unwilling to explore further. As you may have guessed, this is what I would call the unwillingness to unlearn. We go through life defining our knowledge based on what we've learned. Imagine if we defined our knowledge based on what we've unlearned.

Whenever I choose to engage someone on the topic of race, I tend to listen first as I enter such dialogues as the explorer; I explore their theories and conclusions. I explore what led to our having this conversation in the first place, but most of all, I explore how my willingness to explore might impact that person's ability to learn or unlearn and in time become an explorer himself or herself. So I titled this moment "A Curse to Know."

It is with regret that I inform you of a curse that has been put upon us. A curse that allows our progression as a people to die on impact never letting our unity be. It is with great sorrow that I inform you that this curse is generational and transmittable to all who interact with you. You will never know them, and they will never appreciate you. It's an actual curse.

But with the message, I bring an exciting revelation—the know-how to break this curse. Be willing to realize that you don't know the stories of everyone you meet—their histories, their presents, and their futures. To break this curse, you must be willing to learn and unlearn in difficult situations.

Commit to the end of the harm and the beginning of the healing.

Not about Race

I imagine that from time to time, all people are good, brilliant, thoughtful, and willing to love and be loved. I look for those people and hope to engage them.

Before the 2016 presidential primaries got underway, I chatted over social media with a young white woman about race in America. Social media is great for bravery but not for engaging, so I remember that before I hit post. She made a statement I had once heard before and usually ponder its meaning. She stated that before Obama, her best friend, who happened to be black, never thought about race. She never discussed it and evidently did not see color.

Before I reacted to that, I thought carefully, and the first question that came to mind was, *Who was at fault for that? Was it the white friend for thinking her black friend never thought about race?* No, I begged to differ. I told her that it was her black friend's fault for letting her believe she never thought about race.

Letting friends not know who you really are and what engages your consciousness makes you a willing participant in their ignorance, and that can sicken your mind.

I'm Not a Success

Blessed is what I am, success is what I yearn to be.
Unhoused from my home is not what I set out to seek
Unhinged from my people, unthought of from my conscious
The sap of this nectar is not so sweet. Yet its fruit is bitter deep.

A young boy became a young man without my guidance.
Strong without sense, this is my mark to bear.
Knowledge is power, yet this power goes unshared
Yes, I am blessed, but success is what I yearn to be.

If they need lead, should I not come forth?
If tears are to be shed, is not my shirt just a cloth?
If I am willing to abandon my pass, then I am willing to forfeit my future.
I cannot be a success living easy in a land of great hypocrisy.
The shell of a so-called successful Negro man is his ancestor's mockery.

Stay silent, for mockery fits me well.
If I am to tell of my pass, will I be unhoused from my new home, unthought
    of my new conscientious being?
What is due to success, or should I ask, what has success done to me?
No, the grass is not greener on the other side because I come from a place
    with no grass.
No, the cup is not half-full because I have no glass. Yet class kept me
    comfortable.

Blessed is what I am. Success is what I yearn to be.

TERRY LEE WATSON

Where You Gather Strength

With the strength of my ancestor's slave
With the persistence of my civil rights forefathers
With the determination of my father's hustle
With this wisdom I have chosen greatness

My soul and conscious remain stout

With the minds that partakes in knowledge
With the hearts that partakes in love
With the grit that soils the earth with sweat
With this will I have chosen greatness

My soul and conscious remain stout

Where do you gather strength?
From facing the evils of new and old
From revisiting the narratives rarely told
I've gathered the strength of my ancestor's slave.

My soul and conscious remain stout.

The Bridges

Do not underestimate the strong ones; they are the ones who build the
bridges.

The bridges that are meant to fill the gap of inequity, these bridges must
remain intact.

I say it to the naysayers, these bridges may need repairing from time to
time.

As the strong ones may need nourishment for the soul as well.

Do not dismiss the tired ones as their burdens are unknown to you.

Their inability to build or repair the bridge does not mean that they do
not want the bridge to remain strong.

The strength of these bridges is crucial to the tired ones being, 'cause only
then can there be safe passage.

I Can Empathize

I feel even though we were told that we lack compassion.
I love even though this world gives us so much to hate.
I learn even though I was reminded that I was cognitively inferior.
I can still empathize.

I wake even though those around me stay asleep and unconscious.
I speak even though the slave mask has not been removed from my head.
I am the reality. I am my story.
I tell it true no matter how uncomfortable it makes you.
Nevertheless, I still empathize.

Do not take my empathy as complacency.
I still hear, I still know, and I still see.
Don't take my empathy as weakness.
The strength of my Lord has been bestowed upon me.

How Much Is Too Much?

How much racism should a black being tolerate in the land of white
supremacy?
Our humanity is not for bargain or our souls for sale.
We have no obligation to its doctrine or to be slaughtered or chained for
its prosperity.

Who is [she] to ask for our loyalty? Its morality is delinquent 'Merica. It
has not paid it moral dues, nor does it plan on doing so.
We strived in light of and not because of; let this be known to the world.
We owe no answers nor should we plan on giving any.

My mind was sick, and now it's well.
My remedy is the realization of 'Merica's true tale.
She never wanted my conscious to develop because it may bear reason.
And see that all it stands for is simple moral treason.

It seems we're having the same moral problem generation after generation
with very little dialogue or change. To break free from the mental
subjugation of white supremacy, we have to acknowledge its existence and
the role it plays in our comfort.

White supremacy contributes to the comfort of white people as well as
that of all who accept it, and no, I am not just referring to the Uncle Tom or
Sambo character. It has been clear to me that calling white supremacy what
it is stirs confusion as the word *white* tends to act as an adjective. To truly
understand the constitution of white supremacy, you must understand it
from the point of view of those it was meant to oppress, those who openly
and consciously defy its customs, those who consider it the abomination
to democracy that it is.

Not being a white supremacist will never be enough to rid us of its convictions. Yes, you might not contribute to its growth, but you might contribute to its sustainability. I am not here to find fault with or condemn anyone but to reflect a long-lasting condition.

I refuse to condemn any means of resistance to white supremacy period. We as a people have been asked to condemn even when the actions are meant to free us as a people.

I Too Am a Patriot

Blink

My few moments of sanity allow me to reflect on the innocence and the naivety of patriotism. What does it mean for a black man to feel patriotic in the face of white supremacy? I don't possess this patriotic privilege. My patriotic self-derives from the need to feel safe and comfortable in this land, but I understand that this perception of safety is drawn with the ink of fear. How can I allow my sane mind to feel patriotic in the land that calls for my demise? Does the abused feel for their abuser? Am I to accept that the murderer cares for his victim? No, this is neither sensible nor reasonable, so I shall not consider it anymore ... For now.

Patriotism is an internal feeling an individual holds for his or her country, a willingness against all multitudes to consider his or her country as sacred. So for those reasons, I too am a patriot.

I do not see patriotism as someone who does what is expected of him or stands firm when hypocrisy and false opportunity are at my feet. I do not see patriotism as someone who does what is expected of him because it is common practice. I do not see patriotism as a mandatory requirement to bow to one's country or countrymen, to accept its injustice as justice or its oppression as the good of the country.

No, this is not patriotism in the land of the noble free. Those who are willing to stand for what is right must question what is right and question their country and themselves. I have not lived the struggles of my ancestors or the inequalities of my father, but who could claim patriotic greatness if not them? Knocked down and yet they got up. Shot down and yet their spirits calm my inner peace. Who am I to give up on my country when their strength keeps me strong and their preservation keeps me stronger?

For these arguments, I too am a patriot. I refuse to feel like a foreigner in my land of birth, nor do I tend to treat others as strangers in the light of Lady Liberty.

I hold my land accountable for its promise of freedom, and I promise that this land will soon know what freedom is.

My Brother

I had a discussion with my son about the First Amendment. Even at age fourteen, he understands it very well. The conversation took place like so.

Me: "What do you do when someone is using the First Amendment to practice hateful speech?"
Son: "Use my First Amendment right to practice love speech."

How many of you have love speech? Here is my love speech.

Feeling for another, even when your feelings are gone,
Will never replace the magnitude of love or loss of love.

I love you, my brother.
If I want for you, what I want for myself, only then do I want freedom.

Knowing when someone is gone but still in view allows me to take care of my brother.
I want you to be safe, and I want you to be strong. I want you to carry on long after I'm gone.

Learn the difference between agreement and understanding. Support your family; know its institution, and use your intuition to demonstrate reason.

Never live a moment you wouldn't want to be captured forever, my brother.

I love my bother
I respect you as a player and a champion in this game of life. Your voice is loud even in silence.

Use your sound to make waves, your heart to change the beat. Utilize and
    direct the strong, take care of the weak in the streets.

I love you, brother
These are not just words. Let them be known and let them be heard.
But most of all, let them be felt and contagious to boot. My love is not
    surface bound but deep to its roots.

I love you, my sister.
I see you too. Strive, thrive, and no jive. Keep this mother land alive.
Your strength is true, and that's how I see God, through you.

I love you, my sister
A queen with a woven crown. Through all the bullshit, you still remain
    black and proud. So this love is proclaimed and its proclamation is
    loud.

I Am Unapologetic

I can be only who I am, a black man, America.

But never a black man in America, man.

I stand on this podium of truth and unsettled soil.

I hand back your stigma, your judgment, and your expectations.

I am forever sorry, not sorry. I am unapologetic.

My thoughts can't be a hashtag or given a distorted conviction.

I seek not another's ratification, but my gratification comes from being
    unapologetic.

my black skin is not just bound to surface; it is engraved within.

My mind is not a waste, but this land tends to rot.

I'm sorry, not sorry my reality makes you squeamish, I am unapologetic.

I love the word *unapologetic*—not to care what others think of your perception and to show your reality no matter the context. Not to live by what the world's perception of you but instead diligently inform the world of your perception of it. I love all that is and all that is not unapologetic.

Being unapologetic is not making others feel less or threatened but making others feel loved and appreciated. Loved that you are willing and wanting to connect and appreciated because you want that connection to be grounded in your concept of truth.

Being unapologetic is not making others feel uncomfortable; it's acknowledging that there may be moments of discomfort but with the concept of growing together. If I am unapologetic with you, take that as my being vulnerable, not aggressive.

I talk about my sick mind, and I acknowledge its impact. I sat today with a group of folks and discussed what to most would be an uncomfortable yet progressive conversation about race. My awareness of my sick mind has allowed such conversations to become easier, even welcomed. I am able to speak and not apologize for what I say, but I make it clear that what I say comes from a place of love and healing.

The Apology of an Unapologetic Black Man

I live by the notion of sorry, not sorry. For I am unapologetic. Hence, this apology comes from a place not much visited.

To my white brother, I apologize if I ever made you feel like racism was over or just a minor stain on the fabric of our society, as if it were an insignificant culprit in the oppression of my people. Note, my being does not come from Americans' opportunities but from the struggles of my father.

To my white sister, I apologize if I ever made you believe your view on my presence, on my being, impacts my morality or what I think of myself as if my condition, my sense of self depended solely on your portrait of a black man. Note, God made me a black man with all the beauty that comes with that.

To my black brother, I apologize if I made you feel inferior in any way ethnologically mass producing the ideology of white supremacy as if I too were your oppressor instilling the legacy of hate. Note that you are my reason for fighting, my reason for resisting.

To my black queen, my deepest apology I reserve for you. I apologize if I made you feel like you had no voice in a man's world as if to make you feel not beautiful, not wanted, not loved. Note, this is the most single abomination to a black man's conscience.

No acceptance needed.

Walls of Oppression

I recently had a conversation with someone from academia whom I considered a bigwig. Even with bigwigs, I can express only my true being. We engaged in a conversation, and it was said that "People of color enter academia to encourage students of color and to tear down the walls of white supremacy." This was indeed our goal I agreed. "However, academia has a way of creating fires, and as people of color, we find ourselves putting out these fires never having the time to do what we came here to do." Again I agreed. "The sad part is that if allowed to tear down the walls of white supremacy, these fires might not exist in the first place." Pure irony, don't you agree?

As I heard this, I reflected on that faithful day, October 18, 2002. As is the case with any day of extreme misery, such days are easy to recall. I at that time worked as a behavioral specialist and my wife as a retailer. That day, I had a long break between clients and decided to go home to make lunch.

As I pulled into the road on which I lived, I was overwhelmed by fire trucks and a small crowd. I found out that the apartment next door to ours had caught fire and had damaged our place.

That fireman told me exactly what that bigwig told me—To stop the fire from spreading, he had to knock down my wall. Without that, another apartment would have met a similar fate. The problem is that we tend to get fixated on tearing down the wall because we are so focused on the fire. This is understandable, but when will our fixation turn to creating an environment where fires cannot exist?

Your Equilibrium

Someone once asked me why I thought and talked about race so much. My response was simple: "Because you don't talk about it at all. Consider me your equilibrium."

Conversations on race between those who have historically been oppressed and those who have been the oppressor can never be comfortable or equal. Authors such as Baldwin described this as the realization that you rooted for the cowboys as a kid but soon learned you were the Indians being slaughtered. Or Malcolm X who wondered if a rape victim could have feelings for the rapist. Heroes don't mind their story being told, but depicting them as villains is a no-go.

I must again challenge my sane mind to understand that a perpetrator does not want to discuss victimization. Neither do I. This narrative and past narratives are not about victimization due to the brutality in America but about the strength of the people who endured it and still stand.

Long ago, I was bullied until I found myself standing up to the bully. I then became a bully and picked on this African child just as I'd been picked on not long before. As bullied child, I felt that my status could not rise unless I too found a victim.

One day, I picked on this child by making a hitting motion to make him flinch; I planned to hit him when he let his guard down. But on that day, he didn't flinch. He stared at me with eyes that said, *I've seen and survived your wrath, and I'm still here.* I have seen that look. I have given that look. I stopped bullying him and became a bully no more. Even at a young age, I understood that when we oppress a people, violently victimize a people, they will soon fight back. I was wise to realize that. This again has been expressed by many before, but there is something that usually goes unsaid.

The strength of the oppressed is unfathomable. We spend very little time acknowledging the strength that it takes to say, "I'm still here standing after the struggle." When I talk about the impact of racism, I acknowledge the strong ones still here. This is not to say I am ignoring the issues or giving sanctuary to the oppressors or their tactics; I'm taking a moment to point out the perseverance of the unspoken yet diligent victor.

Because of this, I am proud to be your equilibrium.

White Fragility Has Consequences

For the longest time, I have avoided the conversation about white fragility. My unapologetic tendencies did not allow me to consider white fragility as a priority in the discussion of healing wounds. However, as I continue to engage white America on the topic of racism and white supremacy, I have come to understand an elementary truth. So I title this moment "White Fragility Has Consequences."

A young, black college student enters the classroom. He has declared mathematics as his major and is ready to embark on a mission.

"Welcome to calculus. Let's go over the syllabus," the professor says. He looks over the classroom and notices the tall, well-built black student. This student knows he stands out as the professor's more than two-second gaze at him lets the student know that he stands out.

This hypervigilance is nothing new at this time. In fact, it is more than expected. As far back as this young man can remember, his passion, his talent for mathematics, was always met by surprise by white teachers. He had never encountered a math teacher who shared his hue.

In first grade, he was given a math test he finished in less than a minute, and when he turned his examination into the teacher, the teacher responded, "Are you sure you don't want more time to go over your test?" The boy shook his head. The teacher graded his exam in front of him. Check! Check! Check! The boy watched the teacher give a correct mark to each answer. After the last checkmark, the teacher looked at the boy with a semi-puzzled look that slowly turned into a smile.

His eighth-grade math teacher didn't like the boy's confidence in math, and on the final exam, she gave the boy a 99 percent—a 1 percent deduction because in his haste, the boy had misspelled his name. "Don't be so clumsy," the teacher wrote in her notation. He needed a 100 percent on the final to be accepted into honors math in the ninth grade.

In ninth grade, the boy's math teacher noticing his talent for math said, "If you maintain a ninety average in my class, I'll recommend you for honors." She believed in the boy and restored his faith in a discipline that he swore had no confidence in him.

So now here we are in college.

"Okay," the professor says, "How many of you are math majors?"

Multiple hands fly up in the air including the black student's.

"Very well. I am happy to see you all in my class," the professor proclaims cracking a smile.

The black boy could not help but crack a smile too. What an excellent way to be welcomed to a class.

The semester goes on, and like most STEM (science, technology, engineering, and mathematics) courses, group work is part of the syllabus.

"Okay, here are the groups for this year's project," the professor announces. "Make sure to connect and set up times to meet after class."

After class, the young man walks to the board to see whom he is paired up with. He looks down the list, sees his name, and sees the names of three other students. He doesn't recognize the names and assumes they are names of females. He jots down their names and email addresses, stands back, and calls their names out loud. Three white females approach him. Kind gestures are exchanged, and they set up a time to meet.

The Meetings

At their first meeting, the problem given to them by the professor seems straightforward. They decide to meet at one of the girl's dorm's common spaces. With his calculator and a pencil in his ear, he walks over to the residence hall. Pleasantries are exchanged, and now on to the problem. Each expresses his or her opinion on how to solve the problem presented by the professor. One girl is confident that her way is the way to go, another girl agrees with her, and the third has no opinion. Now it's the boy's turn.

"I have a different way of approaching this." The young man is met with looks, not the hypervigilant looks he has become used to; he later finds out it's the "Don't be *that* Negro" look.

They listen to his reasoning but decide his approach is too complicated; they go with the first girl's idea.

Maybe she's right, he thinks. *Her approach does seem simpler, and simple can be good.*

However, this scenario repeats a couple of times. One time, one of the girls looks at him and says, "She's a math major. Maybe we should just let her give us the method."

He looks at her. "I'm a math major too. Maybe we should work as a team to solve the problem."

Silence ...

The math professor walks up to this young man during the next class and asks to see him in his office after class. The boy goes to his office. Pleasantries are exchanged. Where are you from? Where did you get a passion for math? What do you hope to do after you graduate? The young man appreciates his professor's interest in him. Then the reason for the meeting is exposed.

"The reason I am meeting with you is that your team came to me."

They what? he thinks.

"The girls on your team think you're coming off as aggressive. I mean, you're a big black man, and your presence can be ... You know ..."

This once-smiling student is smiling no more. He stares at his professor. "No, I don't know."

"They feel threatened. All I'm saying is tone it down a bit."

"I can maybe adjust my voice and tone, but professor, I will always be a big black man."

The student withdraws from the program never to take a math class again.

Blink

As a black man, I have become aware of how visibility plays into the sickness of America's mind and my own. It is to be depicted as a threat to the white supremacy way of living when I am visible. When I am invisible, it is to hide white supremacy's impact on my mind and well-being. I have no control over the visible threat my skin offers, but I will no longer allow my black skin to remain invisible. I will reveal white supremacy's impact on the consciousness of all people including mine. White fragility has consequences, and these consequences will I swear be known.

Closing in on the Fifth Note

I lay back listening to the brilliance of legendary jazz pianist Oscar Peterson. While most jazz musicians may avoid the fifth note, he so lovingly and it seems effortlessly used it to tempt his listeners. What's next? What's his next run? Back to the fifth note he goes tempting, enticing, and pulling along my ears. Ah, brilliant. The only time I am allowed to breathe is when he finally hits that last chord. Yes, now I can take that breath.

Breathe

When I was in ninth grade, I was part of our concert choral group. I had been part of a choral group since the sixth grade, but I was particularly excited for the spring concert. For days, I practiced and kept a secret from my family that I would be playing the piano in the performance.

My teacher looked at me before I was set to play and gave me a nod. I stepped to the piano, looked over at the shocked expressions of my family, and cracked a smile. The song "Free Willy" sung by Michael Jackson. I played the intro and then the song itself as the choral group sang. "Hold me, like the river Jordan." My heart was pumping. Some of it may have been nerves, but it was because I was so excited to get to the bridge, my favorite part. Especially with a Michael Jackson song. MJ had a way of taking the bridge of a song and really going off. It was a chance for me to show what I could do on the piano with the key changes and do what the bridge was meant to do. Connect the root, the fifth, the rhythm, the emotions, the key change, the excitement for the listener, and lead them to peace. The end. A new end. A changed end. A new root.

Breathe

This final moment is appropriately titled "The Fifth Note." Let me explain the idea of the dominant fifth note. Whenever a song starts, it usually starts on the home note, the first note, especially in most pop music. If it does not, the first note is not far behind, trust me. It is the root of the song. The note on which most of the song will focus. However, before the first verse begins, the note right before the words or melody begins usually hangs the fifth note. Throughout the song, the fifth note will reappear; it is usually followed by the root and before the chorus starts. But what is unique is that this same note will usually be the second to last note of the whole song. When I write a piece, after I identify my root, I identify my fifth.

That got me thinking about this journey of deconstructing white supremacy. What is my fifth note?

Just as brilliant musicians such as Oscar Peterson use the fifth note to inspire listeners, I must use my fifth note to inspire you. I—we—must use our brilliance to inspire our generation and the next to do what is necessary to deconstruct the evil of white supremacy that is upon us.

Just as pianists use the fifth note to inspire the run and the energy that is captured, we can use our ability to run or crawl or walk to our destination keeping in mind all the unique patterns and rhythms that move us and carry us along.

Just as musicians who use the fifth to take us back to the root, we must remember to revisit our root and analyze it before we take on our next run. We must ask ourselves, *Do we keep the same rhythm, or do we improvise our next movement?* How do you plan on using your fifth note?

I mentioned in the beginning moment the crawling, walking, and running from hate that I realized when it comes to the painful walk of America's history. Some people are not ready to walk or even crawl. There is one thing I conveniently left out until now, and that is that they are unable to prepare for the change or the end of the evil that beholds them, that beholds us. Again, that evil I speak of is the legacy of white supremacy.

Just as excitement captured my fourteen-year-old heart and imagination in the ninth grade, we, like musicians, must build up and make strong our bridge. We must connect all that is necessary to do what is necessary. When the bridge comes, just like the key in the song, we must anticipate and be excited about the change. Just like the music, our root should not sound the same after the change which should lead to peace. But through it all, we will still need to play that fifth note.

So my point. If you are an advocate for justice or someone who finds himself or herself fighting, you must ask yourself, *What is my fifth note?* Otherwise, you can never begin your song of equality, or worse, your song may be doomed never to end.

Blink

Welcome to the sick mind of a sane person. As I said, I was born sane. But sometimes, my mind can change like the key in a song. Like a song, my mind can create a bridge between sickness and wellness. The song that is my mind can find its root to sanity as long as I play my fifth note brilliantly leading to the deconstruction of white supremacy. Leading to peace of mind.

Printed in the United States
by Baker & Taylor Publisher Services